The Battle of Jackson, Mississippi

May 14, 1863

Also by Chris Mackowski

Decisions at Fredericksburg: The Fourteen Critical Decisions that Defined the Battle

Grant's Last Battle: The Story Behind the Personal Memoirs of Ulysses S. Grant

The Great Battle Never Fought: The Mine Run Campaign, November 26-December 2, 1863

Hell Itself: The Battle of the Wilderness, May 5-7, 1864

Strike Them a Blow: Battle Along the North Anna River, May 21-25, 1864

Traces of the Bloody Struggle: The Civil War at Stevenson Ridge, Spotsylvania Court House

Chancellorsville's Forgotten Front: The Battles of Second Fredericksburg and Salem Church, May 3, 1863 (with Kristopher D. White)

Don't Give an Inch: The Second Day at Gettysburg, July 2, 1863—From Little Round Top to Cemetery Ridge (with Kristopher D. White and Daniel T. Davis)

Fight Like the Devil: The First Day at Gettysburg, July 1, 1863 (with Kristopher D. White and Daniel T. Davis)

The Last Days of Stonewall Jackson: The Mortal Wounding of the Confederacy's Greatest Icon (with Kristopher D. White)

A Season of Slaughter: The Battle of Spotsylvania Court House, May 8-21, 1864 (with Kristopher D. White)

Seizing Destiny: The Army of the Potomac's "Valley Forge" and the Civil War Winter that Saved the Union (with Albert Z. Conner, Jr.)

Simply Murder: The Battle of Fredericksburg, December 13, 1862 (with Kristopher D. White)

That Furious Struggle: Chancellorsville and the High Tide of the Confederacy, May 1-4, 1863 (with Kristopher D. White)

BATTLES & LEADERS SERIES

The Battle of Jackson, Mississippi
May 14, 1863

Chris Mackowski

Savas Beatie
California

© 2022 Chris Mackowski

Savas Beatie Battles & Leaders Series

All rights reserved. No part of this publication may be reproduced, stored in a retrieval system, or transmitted, in any form or by any means, electronic, mechanical, photocopying, recording, or otherwise, without the prior written permission of the publisher.

First edition, first printing

ISBN-13 (hardcover): 978-1-61121-655-4
ISBN-13 (ebook): 978-1-61121-656-1

Library of Congress Cataloging-in-Publication Data

> Names: Mackowski, Chris, author.
> Title: The Battle of Jackson, Mississippi, May 14, 1863 / by Christopher Mackowski.
> Description: El Dorado Hills, CA : Savas Beatie LLC, [2022] | Series: Savas Beatie battles & leaders series | Includes bibliographical references and index. | Summary: "Drawing on dozens of primary sources, contextualized by the latest scholarship on Grant's Vicksburg campaign, The Battle of Jackson, Mississippi, May 14, 1863, offers the most comprehensive account ever published on the fall of the Magnolia State's capital during Grant's inexorable march on Vicksburg"-- Provided by publisher.
> Identifiers: LCCN 2022011319 | ISBN 9781611216554 (hardcover) | ISBN 9781611216561 (ebook)
> Subjects: LCSH: Jackson, Battle of, Jackson, Miss., 1863 (May 13) | Jackson (Miss.)--History--Siege, 1863. | Vicksburg (Miss.)--History--Siege, 1863. | Mississippi--History--Civil War, 1861-1865.
> Classification: LCC E475.29 .M33 2022 | DDC 973.7/344--dc23/eng/20220314
> LC record available at https://lccn.loc.gov/2022011319

SB

Savas Beatie
989 Governor Drive, Suite 102
El Dorado Hills, CA 95762
916-941-6896 / sales@savasbeatie.com / www.savasbeatie.com

All of our titles are available at special discount rates for bulk purchases in the United States. Contact us for information.

Proudly published, printed, and warehoused in the United States of America.

For Jackson

Table of Contents

Acknowledgments viii

Foreword by Terrence J. Winschel x

Introduction xiii

Chapter 1: Old Joe 1

Chapter 2: Days of Scramble 9

Chapter 3: Hour of Trial Is On Us 19

Chapter 4: The Head-Quarters of Everything 29

Chapter 5: The Decision to Move on Jackson 39

Chapter 6: A Show of Saving the City 47

Chapter 7: Life No Charm, Death No Horror 60

Chapter 8: All Fire and Spirit 78

Chapter 9: Good-Night at the Stars 97

Chapter 10: Destruction of the City 110

Chapter 11: Whose Hearts Should Be as Brothers 124

Chapter 12: The Jackson Battlefield 135

Order of Battle 160

Sources 163

Index 167

About the Author 172

List of Maps

Maps by Edward Alexander

Vicksburg Campaign, March 29–July 4, 1863   xiv

Jackson, MS 1863   30

Johnston's Plan for Pemberton, May 13–14, 1863   54

Battle of Jackson, May 14, 1863   61

Battle of Jackson, May 14, 1863 (Modern Background)   134

Points of Interest, Jackson, MS   136

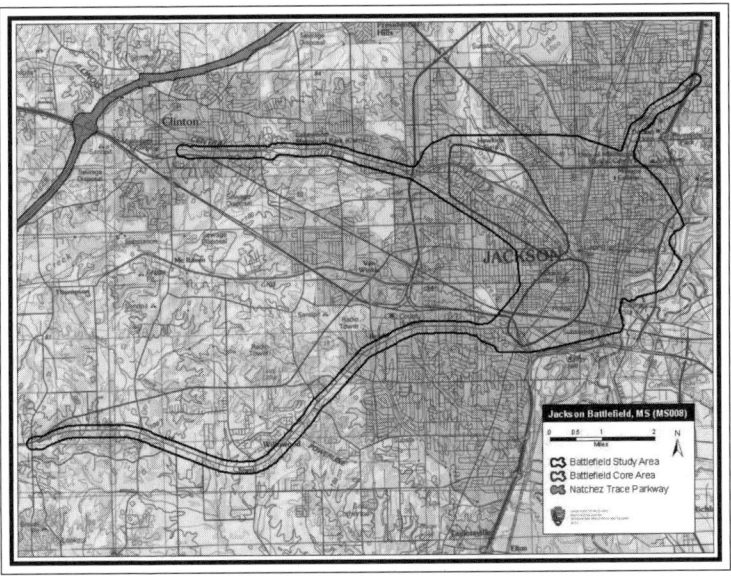

JACKSON BATTLEFIELD, MS

The National Park Service assessment of Jackson's core battlefield areas overlays atop a busy state capital, with virtually no preserved space. The battlefield study area includes the approach routes of the Federal army as well as part of the evacuation route of the Confederates.

National Park Service

Acknowledgments

FIRST, MY thanks to Kris White and the American Battlefield Trust (ABT) for sparking my interest in the Vicksburg Campaign in general and the battle of Jackson specifically. Thanks, too, to Conner Townsend for her excellent work on our expedition.

Dave Powell and Timothy B. Smith looked over early drafts of this manuscript and were gracious with their constructive feedback. I am lucky to count Dave a colleague at Emerging Civil War (ECW) and even luckier to count both Dave and Tim as friends. Dave also helped me track down a few western sources lacking from my eastern-centric library, as did Jon-Erik Gilot and Gary Milligan. Thanks, too, to Pat McCormick for his review of the manuscript.

Matt Atkinson was kind enough to raid the research library at Vicksburg National Military Park for me in search of Jackson-related sources, of which there turned out to be few (not to Matt's surprise). My thanks to Vicksburg National Military Park for giving Matt access for me, though. It's a wonderful park with wonderful resources.

I'm also lucky that when I have a Vicksburg-related question, I can get a quick answer from park historian (and occasional ECW contributor) Andrew Miller or my old friend, historian Emma Murphy Novak. They have been patient with my inquiries, and I appreciate their readiness to always help.

Jim Woodrick was gracious enough to not only offer his expertise but also show me around the lost battlefield of Jackson with the knowing eye of a native and the patience of a sage. I intentionally steered away from the July 1863 actions around the city in my own retelling of Jackson's story because Jim wrote an excellent book on the topic, *The Civil War Siege of Jackson, Mississippi* (History Press, 2016).

Edward Alexander made several great maps that, as usual, enhance the overall work tremendously. At first, I just asked for two . . . then a couple more . . . and finally settled on six. Let's just say that Edward's cartography skills are matched only by his patience.

Publisher extraordinaire Theodore P. Savas continues to give me tremendous latitude with the projects I do. As a creative type, I could not be luckier, really.

At the eleventh hour, Ted surprised me with the news that Terry Winschel, the now-retired historian from Vicksburg National Military Park, was interested in writing a Foreword for me. I sent Terry the manuscript and began to sweat bullets. He is one of the people in the field I most respect and admire, and I was scared to death to disappoint him. Fortunately, he offered a few small edits and some very kind words. I am grateful for his read of the manuscript and for his gracious willingness to write such a great Foreword.

My thanks to my wife, Jenny Ann, who tolerated a lot of late nights of work on my part as this strange project took shape and grew. At some point, it seemed like the Project That Would Not Die, which maybe might have made a great drive-in movie in the 1950s but wasn't so hot on endless replay night after night.

Finally, a shout-out to my kids: to my daughter, Stephanie, her husband, Thomas, and their wonderful little daughter, Sophie Marie (my first grandchild, "The Pip"!); to my youngest son, Maxwell James; and to my oldest son, Jackson, who inspired this whole adventure and to whom this book is dedicated.

FOREWORD
by Terrence J. Winschel

"VICKSBURG IS the key," declared President Abraham Lincoln and asserted that "the war can never be brought to a close until that key is in our pocket." This powerful statement was no exaggeration as Confederate cannon mounted on the bluffs overlooking the Mississippi River at Vicksburg denied that important avenue of commerce to Northern shipping. It was imperative for the administration in Washington to open the river to enable the rich agricultural bounty of the land, especially that of the "Old Northwest," to reach world markets. Pocketing that key would give the North unfettered control of the Mississippi River. It would also divide the South in two, sever major Confederate supply and communications lines, achieve a major objective of the Anaconda Plan, and effectively seal the doom of Richmond. Thus, Vicksburg was a city of unparalleled significance, and the "Gibraltar of the Confederacy" would prove a tough nut to crack.

Throughout 1862 and into 1863 Union land and naval forces made several attempts to capture the city to no avail. Finally, after months of frustration and failure, in the spring of 1863 combined land and naval forces led by Maj. Gen. Ulysses S. Grant and R. Adm. David Dixon Porter launched a campaign that resulted in the fall of Vicksburg on July 4, 1863. Although Grant would later admit that he could not have taken Vicksburg without the navy's assistance, his land operations have been termed "The most brilliant campaign ever waged on American soil." As such, it warrants detailed examination by professional soldiers and students of military history.

Many excellent histories have been written about the campaign at large and even specific aspects of Grant's operations. The battle of Jackson, fought on May 14, 1863, was a key action during the Vicksburg campaign as it resulted in the capture of Mississippi's capital city. More importantly, Union victory scattered Confederate forces under Gen. Joseph E. Johnston to the winds, which provided Grant's force security as he wheeled his Army of the Tennessee west toward its ultimate objective, Vicksburg. It also firmly established Grant's army as a wedge between Lt. Gen. John C. Pemberton's army in Vicksburg and those forces of Johnston that would reoccupy Jackson and pose a threat to Grant's rear throughout the long 47-day siege of the fortress city on the Mississippi River. Grant's position prevented effective communications between the two Confederate generals, keeping them from acting in concert with one another to raise the siege and rescue the beleaguered garrison.

In light of these results, it is hard to understand why most works on the Vicksburg campaign devote but few pages to the battle of Jackson. The lengthiest and most detailed work to date is *The Battle of Jackson May 14, 1863/The Siege of Jackson July 10-17, 1863* (158 pages) by Edwin C. Bearss and Warren Grabau, released by Gateway Press in 1981. This volume is now hard to find and treasured by those who have it. Ed Bearss also included a chapter on the battle of Jackson in Volume II of his trilogy *The Vicksburg Campaign,* recently reprinted by Savas Beatie.

Chris Mackowski, the editor of the *Emerging Civil War* blog, and book series by the same name published by

Savas Beatie, corrects that oversight and fills a significant void in the literature on the campaign with this volume. Mackowski, author or co-author of more than 15 books, focuses his talented pen and marvelous storytelling ability to detail the battle for control of Mississippi's capital city. He combines enough detail to satisfy the serious student of the war and color to appeal to the novice that makes for a smooth-flowing and easy-to-read narrative that is a welcomed addition to the fast-growing field of literature on the Vicksburg campaign.

Terrence J. Winschel
Historian (ret.) Vicksburg National Military Park
Author of the two-volume *Triumph & Defeat:*
The Vicksburg Campaign

Introduction

In May 2018, the American Battlefield Trust (ABT) invited me to visit Mississippi as co-host of a series of Facebook Live videos to commemorate the 155th anniversary of Grant's Vicksburg campaign. I would be traveling with my partner in crime and frequent collaborator, Kris White, the Trust's senior education manager, and Conner Townsend, the Trust's social media manager. Along the way, we'd be joined by Brig. Gen. (ret.) Parker Hills, Timothy B. Smith, Terry Winschel, and historians from the National Park Service as special guests to help share the stories of one of Grant's most impressive feats of the war.

I'm an Eastern Theater guy by background, experience, and proximity, so I had to do some studying up in order to hold my own among such a constellation of western talent. Winschel, retired chief historian of Vicksburg National Military Park, is a legend, and Tim Smith is among the Civil War historians whose work I most admire. I was unfamiliar with Gen. Hills but soon came to appreciate his incredible encyclopedic memory and passion for the story (and I'm lucky that we've since become friends).

I knew in advance I had to pick my battles, so to speak. The Vicksburg campaign was vast, stretching from the city's July 4, 1863, surrender all the way back into the early summer of '62. For our ABT trip, we were focusing

xiv | THE BATTLE OF JACKSON, MISSISSIPPI

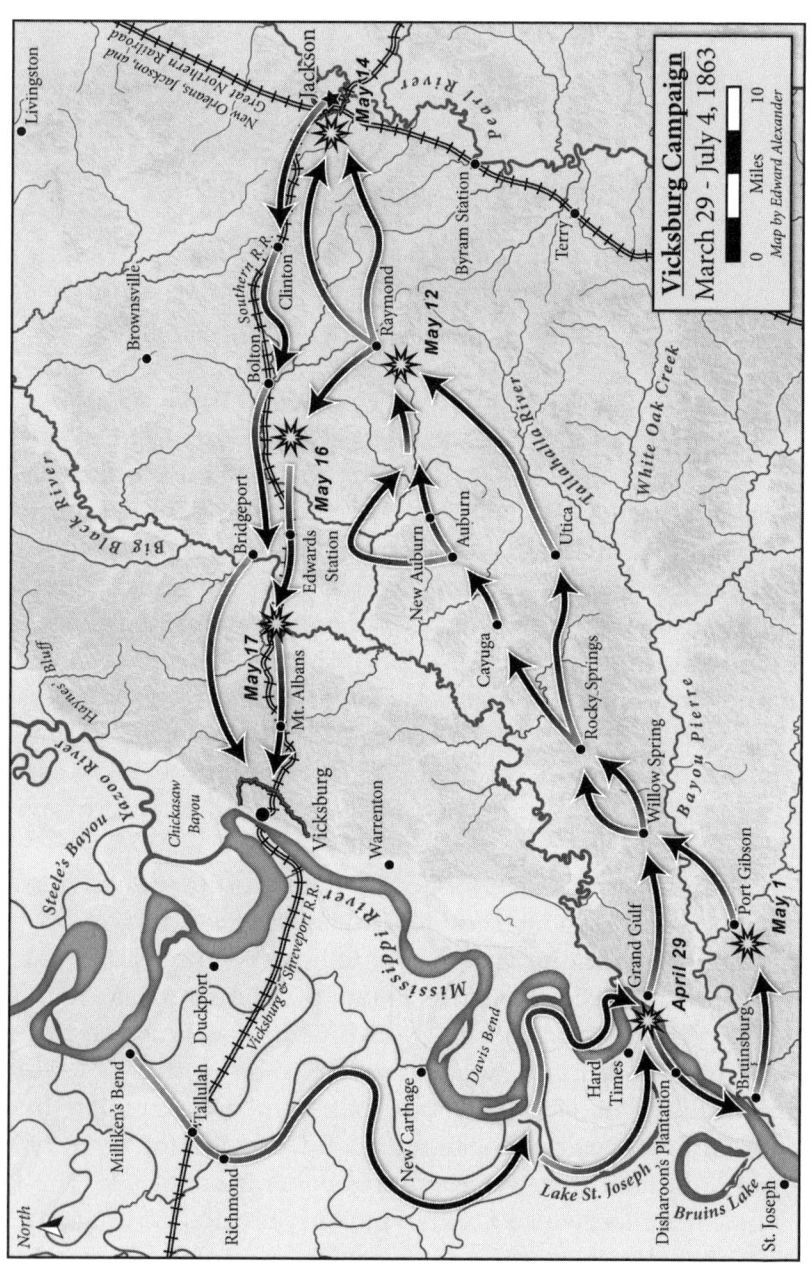

INTRODUCTION | XV

VICKSBURG CAMPAIGN

Some historians have called Grant's overland campaign through Mississippi "the Blitzkrieg of the Civil War." Grant's May 14 capture of Jackson—on the heels of an unimpeded river crossing and successes at Port Gibson, Grand Gulf, and Raymond—set the stage for his pivot west to finally invest Vicksburg by land. Victories at Champion Hill and the Big Black River would bolster Federal confidence prior to assaults on May 19 and 22 and, finally, a 47-day siege. It would also give Grant important insights he would put into play during his 1864 Overland Campaign in Virginia.

Edward Alexander

---

on only the overland actions leading to the gates of the city, as well as the siege itself. If we mark time beginning with the river crossing on April 30, that still manages to encompass 67 days of action, including battles on May 1, 12, 14, 16, 17, 19, and 22, with lots of smaller actions and anecdotes sprinkled in until the surrender of the city on July 4, now famously known as "the most glorious fourth."

For context, let me remind you that I'm a "Stonewall" Jackson fanboy, so the vast majority of my knowledge of events on May 2, 1863, and the eight days that follow are focused on the battle of Chancellorsville, Jackson's accidental wounding by his own men that day, the conclusion of Robert E. Lee's so-called "greatest victory," and Jackson's death on May 10. In that regard, Grant's crossing of the Mississippi could not have been better timed. Like me, most of Richmond's attention was focused on, and absorbed by, events along the Rappahannock, not along the Mississippi. While Jefferson Davis was himself a Mississippian—a resident of Warren County, of which Vicksburg is the county seat—poor health had him laid low by late April, so he struggled to find the energy to deal with the faraway events in his home state when closer events loomed with so much more pressing immediacy.

I set about familiarizing myself as much as possible with the events of those 67 days, padding what I learned with as much additional context as I could. Aside from this breadth, I also wanted to pick something I could go deep on. Aside from their general expertise, I knew Parker would have Raymond covered because he'd personally done so much to preserve that battlefield; I knew Tim would have Champion Hill covered because he wrote "the" book on the battle (and was working on his five-volume magnus opus on the campaign, which has been fantastic); I knew Terry and the NPS folks would have Vicksburg itself covered because of the national military park.

In this context, I chose to become the "instant expert" on the battle of Jackson, although not because of any process of elimination. I chose the battle because my oldest son is named Jackson, christened by his older sister after Stonewall. But even Stonewall Jackson didn't play into my decision, despite my appreciation of him. I did it simply because the battle and my oldest son shared a name.

As I researched the battle of Jackson, news of the fall of the city was almost always preceded, surrounded, and drowned out by news of the fall of the general. This was true in newspapers, diary accounts, and even postwar memoirs. A Google search of "Jackson" in May 1863 (if we can imagine such a thing!) would have certainly returned hundreds if not thousands of lamentations about Stonewall compared to perhaps dozens of mentions of the Mississippi capital. (For kicks, try it yourself: "Jackson + May 1863"). Earl Van Dorn's death at the hands of a jealous husband might make a cameo appearance in the search, too, because he was the one-time commander of the Vicksburg garrison—"Mississippi" might have tripped an algorithm somewhere.

The ABT trip to Mississippi became one of the real highlights of my Civil War career, and my meager attempt to be the crew's expert on the battle of Jackson went smoothly. Kris chuckled at me because, of the two of us, he's usually the one who descends to the microtactical level and I'm usually the big-picture "story" guy, so it amused him to see me go into the weeds.

After the trip, I thought, *I should really do something with all this Jackson research I've done.* I didn't know what, exactly, but I figured I'd get around to writing something at some point. The sheaf of notes, scribbled across pages and pages of yellow ruled paper, sat on a pile on the catch-all top of a filing cabinet next to my desk.

For years.

In 2021, as Emerging Civil War prepared to celebrate its tenth anniversary with a short commemorative series of books, we honed in on Vicksburg as the topic of one of the volumes. *Ah ha!* I thought. *Now's the chance to dust off that research on the battle of Jackson and use it to write an original piece for the Vicksburg volume.* I hadn't revisited the material since the trip, although it didn't take too long to freshen up.

The body of work on the battle of Jackson isn't expansive. Aside from an impossible-to-find short hardcover by Ed Bearss and Warren Grabau written in 1981, no stand-alone work on the battle seemed to exist. (Jim Woodrick, former Civil War historian for the state of Mississippi, has a great little book on the July 1863 siege of Jackson.) Where the battle of Jackson is covered in campaign histories, it typically gets no more than three pages, if that. Even Ed's book covers the battle in a volume that also includes the July siege and three other post-Vicksburg actions.

Here was another chance to go deep.

As my notes took shape in narrative form, that narrative grew and grew. I thought I'd write something hefty in the six-thousand-word range. Then eight thousand. Then suddenly a dozen. And by then, I knew I'd outgrown the ECW Vicksburg volume—and I wasn't even done yet.

What was I going to do with this thing?

During one of my regular conversations with Ted Savas, I mentioned this quandary to him. "Heyyyyy!" he replied. Ted has a way of drawing out the last "y" when he gets a flash of inspiration. "I have an idea. What if we do this. . . ."

And here *this* is.

It will likely take you longer to read about the battle of Jackson than it took the men to fight it. However, I wanted to provide the most comprehensive account to date of the action there. The May 14, 1863, battle does not rank as the most important of Grant's Mississippi campaign, but it does probably rank as the most overlooked. Port Gibson was the first; the fall of Grand Gulf might be the most strategically important; Raymond has had extensive preservation efforts bolstering its story; Champion Hill was easily the most consquential. Perhaps only the flash-in-the-pan fight at the Big Black gets less love than Jackson.

Here, then, is the story of the May 14, 1863, battle of Jackson, Mississippi—with thanks to Kris White and the American Battlefield Trust and inspired, at its very core, by my own son, Jackson.

I assure you, that's a lot of love.

"down through the starlight came the echo of that fainting cry under the wheels of the guns: 'Murder! Murder, boys! Oh, Murder!'"

— *Pvt. Robert Burdette*

1

OLD JOE

JOSEPH E. Johnston was unfit for service and flat-out said so to his boss: "I shall go immediately, although unfit for field service."[1]

But go the general did, departing on May 10, 1863, from Tullahoma, Tennessee, for Jackson, Mississippi, on the peremptory orders of the Confederate Secretary of War, James Seddon. A Union army had made landfall on the east bank of the Mississippi River and was now operating somewhere in the state's interior. Control of the river was at stake. The populace—the white populace, anyway—was panicked. Confederate President Jefferson Davis expressed concern about his home state. Johnston had to go sort things out.

Johnston did not want to make the trip, though—had, in fact, resisted going to Mississippi for months. He had insisted that the Confederate army in middle Tennessee, also under his command, needed his direct supervision more than the army in Mississippi did. He had worried that the commander in Tennessee, Gen. Braxton Bragg, was distracted by the failing health of his dying wife. For good measure, Johnston had also complained that old

---

[1] Johnston to Seddon, 9 May 1863, *The War of the Rebellion: A Compilation of the Official Records of the Union and Confederate Armies* (Washington, D.C.: Government Printing Office, 1889), Series 1. Vol. 23, Pt. 3, 826, hereafter abbreviated as "O.R."

GEN. JOSEPH E. JOHNSTON

One soldier of the Army of Tennessee described Joe Johnston thus: "Fancy, if you please, a man about fifty years old, rather small of stature but firmly built, an open countenance, and a keen, restless eye that seemed to read your inmost thoughts. In his dress he was a perfect dandy. He ever wore the finest clothes that could be obtained, carrying out in dress and the paraphernalia of the soldier the plan adopted by the War Department at Richmond, never omitting anything, even to the trappings of his horse, bridle and saddle. His head was decorated with a star and feather, his coat with every star and embellishment, and he wore a bright new sash, big gauntlets, and silver spurs. He was the very picture of a general."

Library of Congress

war injuries still ailed him, thus making him too unwell to serve in the field.

The thing Johnston worried about most, though, was his reputation. His litany of complaints served primarily as a smokescreen to defend it.

"[O]ld Joe was a yerker," said Pvt. Sam Watkins of the Army of Tennessee admiringly. "He took all the tricks. He was a commander."[2] Arthur Fremantle, a British colonel observing the American war in the spring and summer of 1863, was impressed by the "commander's" bearing:

> In appearance, General Joseph E. Johnston, commonly called Joe Johnston, is rather below the middle height, spare, soldierlike, and well set up; his features are good, and he has lately taken to wear a grayish beard. He is a Virginian by birth, and appears to be about fifty-[six] years old. He talks in a calm, deliberate, and confident manner; to me he was extremely affable, but he certainly possesses the power of keeping people at a distance when he chooses and his officers evidently stand in great awe of him.[3]

As a career officer, Johnston had an impressive resume that he'd begun building during the war with Mexico decades earlier. After, he served with distinction in the antebellum army and, when civil war broke out, became the highest-ranking officer to defect to the Confederacy. A disagreement over how to count that pre-war service when it came time to issue ranks in the Confederate army led to a dispute between Johnston and President Davis: Johnston fell behind Samuel Cooper, Albert Sidney Johnston, and Robert E. Lee on the list of seniority but

---

2 Sam Watkins, *Co. Aytch: A Side Show of the Big Show*, 2nd ed. (Chattanooga, TN: Times Printing Company, 1900), 106.

3 Arthur Fremantle, *Three Months in the Southern States* (London: William Blackwood and Sons, 1863), 116.

CONFEDERATE PRESIDENT
JEFFERSON DAVIS

A native of Mississippi, Jefferson Davis owned a plantation on the outskirts of Vicksburg—as did his brother, Joseph—so the military situation along the river was not only of vital national importance to him but also of keen personal interest.

Library of Congress

thought he should rank higher. His placement in the number-four slot "seeks to tarnish my fair fame as a soldier and a man, earned by more than thirty years of laborious and perilous service," he complained.[4] Slighted, the too-proud Johnston held a grudge against Davis that ever thereafter poisoned their relationship. "His hatred of Jeff Davis amounts to a religion," diarist Mary Chesnut would write of the embittered Virginian. "With him it colors all things."[5] Indeed, says scholar Stephen Cushman with the benefit of a century and a half of hindsight, "The two men did not trust, cooperate with, or forgive each other as long as they lived."[6]

Nonetheless Johnston was one of the Confederacy's true war heroes after earning victory at First Manassas in July 1861 (though, in fact, he had little to do with it). He remained in command of Confederate forces in his native Virginia through May 31, 1862, when a shell fragment knocked him out of action at the battle of Seven Pines. This was the war wound he would thereafter milk whenever called on to perform a task he didn't want to do.

Davis had disapproved of Johnston's strategy during the spring campaign on the Virginia Peninsula and, in fact, Johnston's wounding must've seemed at least a partial relief to the Confederate commander in chief. Robert E. Lee's subsequent success as Johnston's replacement made the switch permanent. As much as Johnston wanted his old army back, Davis had no intention of replacing Lee, even after Johnston had recuperated. Rechristened the Army of Northern Virginia, it was Lee's army in spirit as well as in fact, and "Old Joe" would ever after be on the outs.

---

4   Johnston to Davis, 12 September 1861, O.R., series IV, Vol. I, 607.

5   Mary Boykin Chestnut, *A Diary from Dixie*, Isabella Martin and Myrta Lockett Avary, eds. (New York: D. Appleton and Company, 1905), 248-49.

6   Stephen Cushman, "Joseph E. Johnston," *Essential Civil War Curriculum*, https://www.essentialcivilwarcurriculum.com/joseph-e.-johnston.html (accessed 10 January 2021).

To solve the problem, Davis promoted Johnston to command of the Western Theater—from the Appalachian Mountains to the Mississippi River. A position of high stakes required a skilled commander, and like many others, Davis respected Johnston's reputation even if he did not like the man or approve of his spring performance on the Peninsula. Of the tools available, Johnston seemed best equipped to handle the vast responsibility in the West. "Whatever man can do will be done by him," Davis would tell Mississippi lawmakers, expressing "perfect confidence."[7]

Johnston, for his part—with bruises to his ego to nurse—believed Davis promoted him as an elaborate ruse to set him up for failure. "[T]he forces . . . under my command are greatly inferior in number to those of the enemy opposed to them," he wrote, sounding much like his old nemesis, Union Maj. Gen. George McClellan, who habitually overestimated enemy strength.[8] Worse, in Johnston's opinion, the geographic expanse under his charge was too vast to cover with the troops available to him. He sought on several occasions to consolidate the two main armies in the theater, Bragg's Army of Tennessee and Lt. Gen. John Pemberton's Army of Vicksburg. Davis refused, instead ordering Johnston to establish a headquarters that "in his judgment will best secure facilities for ready communication with the troops within the limits of his

---

7   Jefferson Davis, speech to Mississippi legislature, 26 December 1862. From Rice University's online Papers of Jefferson Davis. https://jeffersondavis.rice.edu/archives/documents/jefferson-davis-speech-jackson-miss-0 (accessed 3 March 2021). Text from *The Papers of Jefferson Davis*, Volume 8, 565-84, transcribed from the 29 December 1862 edition of the Memphis *Appeal*, which, according to *The Papers*, was being published in Jackson at that time.

8   Joseph E. Johnston, *Narrative of Military Operations, Directed, During the Late War Between the States, by Joseph E. Johnston* (New York: D. Appleton and Company, 1874), 149.

command. . . ." Wherever headquarters turned out to be, Johnston's orders explicitly stated that he should not feel tethered to the spot but rather "repair in person to any part of said command whenever his presence may for the time be necessary or desirable."[9]

From Davis's perspective, Richmond was too far from both Tennessee and Mississippi, and "he thought it necessary to have an officer nearer, with authority to transfer troops from one army to another in an emergency," as Johnston later explained. "If such an officer was needed," he continued, "I certainly was not the proper selection; for I had already expressed the opinion that such transfers were impracticable, because each of the two armies was greatly inferior to its antagonist; and they were too far from each other for such mutual dependence."[10]

Johnston thus set up shop in central Tennessee and thereafter did his best to pretend the Vicksburg army wasn't really his concern. "The only effect . . . of my taking direction of affairs," he wrote a political ally, "would be my being responsible for Pemberton's generalship, instead of himself. If he entitled himself to praise, robbing him of it. If he deserves blame, bearing it for him."[11]

Whenever Richmond pressed him, Johnston responded with his smokescreen of concerns, complaints, and ailments. By early April, when Bragg's wife's health recovered and Johnston no longer had that distraction as an excuse, he "afterward became sick" himself and, as he reported to Jefferson Davis on April 10, "am not

---

9 Special Orders 275, 24 November 1862, O.R. XVII, 758.

10 Johnston, *Narrative*, 154-55.

11 Joseph Johnston to Louis Wigfall, 8 March 1863, quoted in John R. Lundberg, "I Am Too Late," *The Vicksburg Campaign, March 29-May 18, 1863*, Steven E. Woodworth and Charles D. Grear, eds. (Carbondale, IL: Southern Illinois University Press, 2013), 119.

now able to serve in the field."[12] Sympathetic biographer Craig L. Symonds describes Johnston as "suffering from incompletely healed wounds, exacerbated now by his frequent travels," adding apologetically that Johnston exercised only "nominal command."[13] Historian John Lundberg counters that "Johnston used his discomfort as a cover for not pursuing his command in Mississippi more proactively."[14]

But on May 10, 1863, with a Federal army under Maj. Gen. Ulysses S. Grant driving boldly through Mississippi's interior, Johnston had no choice but to go west.

---

12 Johnston to Davis, 10 April 1863, O.R. XXII, Pt. 2, 745.

13 Craig L. Symonds, *Joseph E. Johnston: A Civil War Biography* (New York: W.W. Norton & Co., 1992), 201.

14 Lundberg, 120.

2

Days of Scramble

GRANT HAD been haranguing Mississippi for months, with little yet to show for it. His efforts focused on Vicksburg, the so-called "Gibraltar of the Confederacy," which sat atop high bluffs overlooking the Mississippi River. Vicksburg connected the eastern half of the Confederacy with much-needed supplies from its Trans-Mississippi region to the west, "the nail head that holds the South's two halves together," as Davis called it.[1] The city's bluff-top defenses also impeded free Federal transport along the river. As a result, U.S. President Abraham Lincoln had targeted the city. "Vicksburg is the key," Lincoln asserted.[2]

Beginning in late 1862, Grant tried on six separate occasions to take Vicksburg or circumvent its grip on the river, all to no avail. Rather than replace his general, though, Lincoln recognized his tenacity. "[I]f Grant only does one thing down there," he vowed, "I don't care much how, so long as he does it right—why, Grant is my man and

---

1 Quoted ubiquitously, but here taken from Terrence Winschel, *Vicksburg: Fall of the Confederate Gibraltar* (Abilene, TX: McWhitney Foundation Press, 1999), 14.

2 David Dixon Porter, *Incidents and Anecdotes of the Civil War* (New York: D. Appleton and Company, 1885), 95-6.

10 | THE BATTLE OF JACKSON, MISSISSIPPI

MAJ. GEN. ULYSSES S. GRANT

Ulysses S. Grant had tried fruitlessly for months to get at Vicksburg. With political pressure mounting against him, his campaign into the Mississippi interior represented perhaps his last chance to make something happen — and he did.

Library of Congress

"Crossing the Mississippi river, we landed at Bruinsburg," wrote a member of McPherson's Corps, "and left that place . . . marching twelve miles over dusty roads and through a hilly and broken country. Although the boys were tired, their minds were diverted with the scenery of a new State."

A Soldier's Story of the Siege of Vicksburg

I am his the rest of the war!"[3] Not that time was infinite. Grant's direct superior, General in Chief Henry Halleck, prodded continually. "[T]he President . . . seems to be rather impatient about matters on the Mississippi . . ." Halleck wrote on April 1.[4] Indeed, by that point, Lincoln's patience had begun to waver.

For attempt number seven, Grant marched his army along the Louisiana side of the Mississippi to a point south of Vicksburg called Hard Times Plantation—a distance of sixty miles for some of the soldiers. Federal naval vessels from the upper Mississippi then ran the gauntlet past the city and linked up with Grant. On April 30, the navy

---

3 Brooks D. Simpson, *Ulysses S. Grant: Triumph Over Adversity, 1822-1865*, (New York: Houghton Mifflin, 2000), 215.

4 Halleck to Grant, 2 April 1863, O.R. XXIV, Pt. 1, 25.

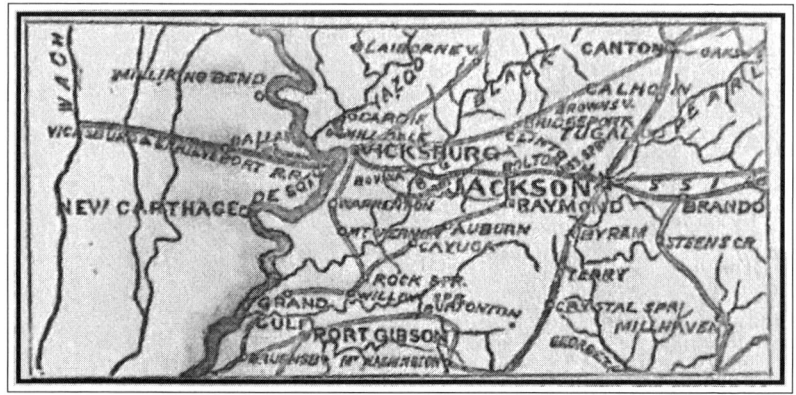

The converging railroads made Jackson a vital transportation hub. This historic map shows the state capital as it relates to Vicksburg as well as Grant's overall area of operation.

Author's collection

---

shuttled Grant's army from west bank to east, depositing them in Bruinsburg.[5]

On May 1, Grant marched a few miles inland and scored a victory at Port Gibson, and on May 3 he flushed out a Confederate garrison at Grand Gulf. "[F]rom Grand Gulf there is a good road to Jackson and the Black River Bridge without crossing the Black River," he'd told Halleck the previous month, mapping out the most practical overland route to avoid the bayous and mires closer to the river. "This is the only move I now see as practicable . . ." he'd decided.[6]

In the wake of Grant's Port Gibson victory, Pemberton—who had headquartered himself in Jackson—relocated to Vicksburg in an attempt to better position himself and consolidate his forces. Grant's attempts against the city

---

5 This would constitute the largest amphibious assault conducted by the U.S. army until the landings in North Africa in WWII.

6 Grant to Halleck, 4 April 1863, O.R. XXIV, Pt. 1, 25-6.

over the previous months, and maneuvers he conducted to cover his march to Hard Times, had left Confederates widely scattered. "If Grant's army lands on this side of the river," Johnston had wired Pemberton from Tullahoma on May 1, "the safety of Mississippi depends on beating it. For that object you should unite your whole force."[7] Pemberton sent out a flurry of telegrams, recalling as many men as he could find. He ordered "all intrenching tools and axes . . . to be collected and turned over" so the city's defenses could be strengthened.[8] He wired to Richmond to plead for reinforcements. "The stake is a great one," he told Seddon. "I can see nothing so important."[9] Davis himself responded the next day: "You may expect whatever is in my power to do."[10]

Publicly, Davis offered nothing but support for Pemberton but, privately, he had begun to have misgivings, at least in regards to the overall situation along the Mississippi if not about Pemberton directly.[11] Mississippians did not make that distinction. They distrusted Pemberton, a Pennsylvanian married to the Confederate cause because his wife was a native Southerner. "The people with this dept., soldiers and citizens, do not repose that confidence in the capacity and loyalty of Genl. Pemberton, which is so important at this junction, whether justly or not . . ." wrote the editors of the Jackson *Mississippian* in a private letter to Davis on May 8. "[F]ears are daily expressed by leading influential

---

7   Johnston to Pemberton, 1 May 1863, O.R. XXIV, Pt. 3, 808.

8   Special Orders 150, 4 May 1863, O.R. XXIV, Pt. 3, 831.

9   Pemberton to Seddon, 6 May 1863, O.R. XXIV, Pt. 3, 838.

10 Davis to Pemberton, 7 May 1863, O.R. XXIV, Pt. 842.

11 Michael B. Ballard, *Pemberton: A Biography* (Jackson, MS: University Press of Mississippi, 1991), 153.

LT. GEN. JOHN C. PEMBERTON

The "Peter Principle" might well have been called the "Pemberton Principle" after the ill-fated John C. Pemberton, who rose to his level of incompetence when he took command in Vicksburg.

Library of Congress

men . . ." the editors warned; "and this feeling prevails to an alarming extent in the army and among our people."[12]

"Your dispatch is the more painful because there is no remedy . . ." a regretful Davis admitted in his reply. "The distrust surprises me and is surely unjust. Try to correct it, for our country's sake."[13]

The editors had already tried, though, as they pointed out in their letter. "The Mississippian has never encouraged these apprehensions," they stressed, "but endeavors on all occasions to allay them and instill perfect confidence in their commanders." In fact, that very week, a notice appeared in the paper that could be described as nothing short of boosterism:

> Let any man who questions the ability of Gen. Pemberton only think for a moment of the condition the department was in when he was first sent here. No General has evinced a more sleepless vigilance in the discharge of his duty, or accomplished more solid and gratifying results. . . . For our part, we are perfectly willing to trust to the plans and executions of our Generals. They know more than we do. Our duty is to assist them to our utmost ability and to trust them. Let every man do his duty.[14]

The editors well knew the value of toeing the Confederate line. They saw it as their patriotic duty to express their concerns only privately, although surely Davis wondered how long it would be before those same concerns appeared in the newspaper itself. The sour public opinion coupled with the opaquely unfolding military events to create

---

12 Cooper and Kimball to Davis, 8 May 1863, O.R. LII, Vol. 2, 468-9. For being newspaper editors, Cooper and Kimball had atrocious punctuation, so I've added commas to their quote to improve readability.

13 Ibid, in Davis's endorsement to the Cooper/Kimball letter.

14 Quoted in the *Montgomery* (AL) *Daily Mail*, 16 May 1863, 1.

"intense anxiety over Pemberton's situation," says Davis biographer William C. Davis.[15]

"Send us a man we can trust," the *Mississippian* editors pleaded to the president, "Beauregard, Hill or Longstreet & confidence will be restored & all will fight to the death for Miss."

Davis's glum answer must have disappointed. "Time does not permit the change you propose," he told them. Instead, he sent them Johnston—"to avail ourselves of the public confidence felt in his military capacity," as he later said.[16]

As these days of scramble unfolded, though, Johnston remained content to armchair-general from Tennessee. "If Grant crosses, unite all your troops to beat him," he unhelpfully ordered Pemberton on May 2, basically repeating himself from the day before.[17] He asked for details about Confederate dispositions, movements, and plans, but Pemberton couldn't even seem to get a clear picture for himself, nor could he get a clear picture of what Grant was up to.

Finally came the morning dispatch from Richmond on May 9 ordering Johnston to find out for himself what exactly was going on in the western part of his department. "Proceed at once to Mississippi and take chief command of the forces, giving to those in the field, as far as practicable, the encouragement and benefit of your personal direction . . ." Seddon's telegram said. "You will find re-enforcements from General [P. G. T.] Beauregard to General Pemberton, and more may be expected."[18]

---

15 Quoted in William C. Davis, *Jefferson Davis: The Man and His Hour* (New York: Harper Collins, 1991), 501.

16 Jefferson Davis, *The Rise and Fall of the Confederate Government,* Vol. 2 (London: Longmans, Green and Co., 1881), 403.

17 Johnston to Pemberton, 2 May 1863, O.R. XXIV, Pt. 3, 815.

18 Seddon to Johnston, 9 May 1863, O.R. XXIII, Pt. 2, 825-6.

BRIG. GEN. EVANDER MCNAIR
During the war with Mexico, Evander McNair served in the 1st Mississippi Rifles under Col. Jefferson Davis.

Library of Congress

Seddon also authorized Johnston to take reinforcements with him from Bragg's army. As Johnston prepared for departure, Bragg detailed two brigades to follow in Johnston's wake: a brigade of Texans under Brig. Gen. Matthew D. Ector and a brigade of Arkansans under Brig. Gen. Evander McNair.[19] McNair, as it happened, had once lived in Jackson and operated a mercantile there from 1842-1856 before moving to Arkansas.[20] The two brigades received orders to cook up three days' rations and march to Wartrace, just outside the army's encampment in Shelbyville, where they would board trains for the trip to Mississippi. On May 11, for good measure, Bragg also detailed the 29th and 60th North Carolina infantry to follow. The Tar Heels marched to the depot in Shelbyville to entrain for the trip west except for the regiment's sick and wounded, shuttled to Atlanta to convalesce.[21] All told, Johnston led the way for 3,500 troops, three batteries, and 2,000 cavalry, who would all follow in his wake, with 6,000 more—Maj. Gen.

---

19 Jack to Stewart, 9 May 1863, O.R. XXII, Pt. 2, 826.

20 Robert Patrick Bender, "Evander McNair," *Encyclopedia of Arkansas*, https://encyclopediaofarkansas.net/entries/evander-mcnair-7851/ (accessed 9 March 2021).

21 Jack to Stewart, 11 May 1863, O.R. XXII, Pt. 2, 829, 830.

John C. Breckinridge's division—ordered to join them later in the month.[22]

Johnston left Tullahoma on May 10 and arrived in Jackson three days later after a circuitous route that took him through Atlanta and Montgomery. And then, almost immediately, he fired off a note to Richmond—"I am too late"—sounding almost as peremptory as the order that had sent him to Jackson in the first place.

Too late, indeed. Grant, having continued his overland campaign through the Mississippi interior, was suddenly looming on the outskirts of the state capital.

---

22 Bragg to Davis, 23 May 1863, O.R. XXII, Pt. 2, 848.

3

Hour of Trial is On Us

THE LAST time Joe Johnston had been in Jackson had been the previous December and January as part of an inspection tour with Jefferson Davis. During the trip, the general and his commander-in-chief spent considerable time discussing but not resolving their philosophical differences on strategy. Davis advocated a defense of key geographical positions along the river, what he would describe as "the vital issue of holding the Mississippi at Vicksburg."[1] Johnston, on the other hand, sought to consolidate troops for mobility; he was willing to give up territory to preserve his combat forces. The disparity between the two men sat at the crux of Johnston's dissatisfaction with his assignment—and its irreconciliation would bode ill for the eventual events of spring.

Davis took time on the Mississippi trip for more pleasant activities than talks with his disgruntled department chief, including a visit to his home and his brother's, the purchase of additional land, and, on the day after Christmas, the delivery of an address at the Mississippi state house. "Wherever duty may have called me," he assured lawmakers of his home state, "my heart has been with you. . . ."[2]

---

1 Davis to Bragg, 22 May 1863, O.R. XXII, Pt. 2, 847.

2 Davis, speech to legislature.

Sketched by Alfred Waud in 1866, Jefferson Davis's home at Davis Bend, Brierfield, was located about twenty miles south of Vicksburg. Fire destroyed the building in 1931, but prior to that, it enjoyed a postwar life as a tourist attraction, with the phrase "The house that Jeff built" painted on the front.

The Rise and Fall of the Confederate Government

While that promise might have been true for his heart, it was not so for his attention, as events soon demonstrated. In mid-April, Davis's health collapsed, leaving him bedridden well into May. Unable to visit the office, he tried from his sickbed to maintain what biographer William C. Davis characterized as his "vast correspondence," but with only moderate success. Normally a notorious micromanager, the Confederate president was notably quieter during this span. Biographer Davis called him "strangely uninvolved" and "almost entirely a passive observer. . . ."[3]

That's all the more remarkable for the series of military events that began to unfold in late April. Along

---

3   William C. Davis, *Jefferson Davis*, 499, 500, 502.

HOUR OF TRIAL IS ON US | 21

The May 1863 deaths of Confederate generals Earl Van Dorn (left) and Thomas "Stonewall" Jackson (right) proved major distractions to Jefferson Davis at the very time he needed to focus on Grant's move into Mississippi.

Library of Congress/Library of Congress

the Mississippi, Grant started to move, but to what end appeared initially unclear. Then, just fifty miles north of Richmond, the Federal Army of the Potomac stirred to life and, on the first four days of May, grappled with the Army of Northern Virginia at a small wilderness crossroads known as Chancellorsville. While Lee's army ultimately won, it did so at the cost of some thirteen thousand troops and the serious wounding of Lee's Second Corps commander, the legendary Thomas Jonathan "Stonewall" Jackson. Like the rest of the South, Davis held worried vigil waiting for news of Jackson's fate. Even as that tragedy unfolded, word arrived from Spring Hill, Tennessee, that lothario Gen. Earl Van Dorn—Pemberton's predecessor at Vicksburg—had been gunned down by a lover's jealous husband. Van Dorn and Davis had been old friends. Elsewhere in Tennessee, bickering between Braxton Bragg and his officers began boiling over again. In Richmond and from around the Confederacy, political trouble always stirred, and April bread riots in the capital remained fresh in Davis's mind.

Secretary of War Seddon's frail health was only marginally better than Davis's that spring, but his was a chronic condition, so he seemed better able to roll with the ups and downs and so picked up much of Davis's slack. He understood the strategic necessity of the Vicksburg defense and focused considerable energy on finding additional troops to send west. As early as April 6, he tried prying troops away from the Army of Northern Virginia, wondering aloud whether "two or three brigades, say of Pickett's division" could be spared. "[T]hey would be an encouraging re-enforcement to the Army of the West," he told army commander Robert E. Lee.[4] Maj. Gen. George Pickett's division was one of two—Maj. Gen. John Bell Hood's being the other—on detached duty from the army for a foraging mission in southeast Virginia.

Lee demurred. "The most natural way to reinforce Genl Johnston would seem to be to transfer a portion of the troops from this department to oppose those sent west," he admitted, "but it is not as easy for us to change troops from one department to another as it is for the enemy, and if we rely on that method we may be always too late."[5] The two continued tugging back and forth over the issue, although Seddon chose not to push too hard. The transfer of even just Pickett's division would mean 7,500 much-needed men.

As it happened, Lt. Gen. James Longstreet—Pickett's commander and one of the very men the editors of the *Mississippian* had called for—also supported a move to

---

4   Seddon to Lee, 6 April 1863, O.R. XXV, pt. 2, 709.

5   Lee to Seddon, 9 April 1863, O.R. XXV, pt. 2, 713-714.

JAMES SEDDON
The Confederacy's Secretary of War, James Seddon, tried to shift troops from the Army of Northern Virginia to Mississippi, but he became just one more person Robert E. Lee would out-maneuver.

National Archives

the west in support of Vicksburg. "I thought that honor, interest, duty, and humanity called us to that service," Longstreet later said.[6]

Rather than send troops to Mississippi to move against Grant directly, though, Lee's Old Warhorse suggested a concentration of reinforcements in middle Tennessee—reinforcements that would include Hood and Pickett, with Longstreet himself along for good measure. Joe Johnston, in overall command of that force, could then combine with Braxton Bragg's Army of Tennessee and move against Maj. Gen. William Starke Rosecrans's Army of the Cumberland in Murfreesboro. "The combination once made should strike immediately in overwhelming force upon Rosecrans, and march for the Ohio River and Cincinnati," Longstreet argued.[7] Such an invasion would force a Federal response, he concluded, and "Grant's was the only army that could be drawn on to meet this move, and that the move must, therefore, relieve Vicksburg."[8]

---

6 James Longstreet, *From Manassas to Appomattox: Memoirs of the Civil War in America* (Philadelphia: J.B. Lippincott Co., 1896,) 331.

7 Ibid.

8 Ibid 327.

Lee's victory at Chancellorsville—and the 13,000 killed, wounded, and missing Confederates that resulted—changed the calculus. "Unless we can obtain some reinforcements," Lee wrote to Seddon on the early afternoon of May 10, "we may be obliged to withdraw into the defenses around Richmond. We are greatly outnumbered now. . . . The strength of this army has been reduced by the casualties of the late battles."[9]

Earlier in the day, Lee had sent a brief note that laid out the situation in the starkest possible terms: "it becomes a question between Virginia and the Mississippi." Davis, seeing the note, told Seddon, "The answer of General Lee was such as I should have anticipated, and in which I concur."[10] Concurring with Lee's assessment did not necessarily mean he concurred with Lee's priorities, though.

Seddon took Lee's note as a final "no"—and, indeed, the army commander would come to Richmond on May 15 to pitch his idea for what would become the Gettysburg campaign as his alternative to sending troops to Mississippi. Lee was "averse to having a part of his army so far beyond his reach," Longstreet later admitted, and the Virginia-centric commander looked for a way to use the men himself rather than send them away.[11] He even tried to get reinforcements of his own, poached from Maj. Gen. D. H. Hill's department in North Carolina, rather than loan any of his own men out.

Unable to draw reinforcements from Lee's army, Seddon turned to Gen. P. G. T. Beauregard's forces in South Carolina. On May 2, aware that Grant was "concentrating great forces on the Mississippi," Seddon wired to Beauregard to send "with the utmost dispatch 8,000 or 10,000 men . . . to General Pemberton's relief."

---

9   Lee to Seddon, 10 May 1863, O.R. XXV, pt. 2, 790.

10 Lee to Seddon, 10 May 1863, O.R. XXV, pt. 2, 790.

11 Longstreet, 328.

GEN. P. G. T. BEAUREGARD As the man who fired the war's first shot, P. G. T. Beauregard secured a reputation for himself as a legitimate Southern hero, but he failed to impress President Jefferson Davis, who held Beauregard in increasing disdain as the war progressed.

National Archives

That included the diversion of men originally intended for Tullahoma.[12] Beauregard complied —sort of—but he worried, "To reduce this command further might become disastrous."[13]

On May 6, the 46th Georgia, 16th and 24th South Carolina, 8th Georgia Battalion, and Capt. Thomas Ferguson's South Carolina Battery assembled under the command of Brig. Gen. States Rights Gist and marched to Charleston's train depot on Mary Street. They loaded themselves onto freight and flat cars in four sections for what would be eight days and seven nights of travel to Jackson, transferring tents and baggage from train to boat and back again a total of six times. "Along the entire route they were greeted at every station by the people, who saluted them by waving flags, handkerchiefs, and by every expression of patriotic approval," a historian for the 24th South Carolina later wrote. "The men and officers, crowded into unclean baggage cars or on open flats, were cheerful and exultant,

12 Seddon to Beauregard, 2 May 1863, O.R. XIV, 923.

13 Beauregard to Seddon, 3 May 1863, O.R. XIV, 924.

and responded to the enthusiasm of the people by waving their hats and cheering lustily at every stop."[14]

Beauregard likewise wired to Savannah, also within his department, and assembled the 25th, 29th, and 30th Georgia, the 1st Georgia Sharpshooter Battalion, the 4th Louisiana Battalion, and Capt. Robert Martin's Georgia Battery, with Brig. Gen. W. H. T. Walker in command. They, too, entrained on May 6 for a journey west.

"I have sent to you two brigades of my troops . . . having selected the best that could be spared, under two of my ablest generals," Beauregard telegraphed Pemberton. All told, the numbers totaled about 5,000 men, including Beauregard's own son, René, a lieutenant in Ferguson's Battery. "I only regret I could not send you double the number," Beauregard added, conveniently ignoring the fact Seddon had specifically ordered him to do just that. He concluded with a wish for "ample success."[15] Seddon did try to pry another 5,000 men from him, but the Creole general would not budge.[16] Not until a peremptory special order on May 15 did Brig. Gen. Nathan G. "Shanks" Evans's brigade proceed toward Jackson—by then too late to be of any help to the Mississippi capital.

Beauregard's prompt if numerically challenged response illuminates an important aspect of Lee's demurral. "If you determine to send Pickett's division to Genl Pemberton," Lee told Seddon on May 10, "I presume it would not reach him until the last of this month. If anything is done in that quarter, it will be over by that time, as the climate in June will force the enemy to retire. The uncertainty of its arrival and the uncertainty of its application cause me

---

14 Walter B. Capers, *The Soldier-Bishop, Ellison Capers* (New York: The Neale Publishing Company, 1912), 60-1.

15 Beauregard to Pemberton, 5 May 1863, O.R. XXIV, Pt. 3, 833.

16 See correspondence between Beauregard and Seddon through pg. 944 in O.R. XIV.

RENE BEAUREGARD
Here photographed in his later years, Rene Beauregard, son of P. G. T. Beauregard, was among the troops the Creole general sent to Jackson.

Library of Congress

to doubt the policy of sending it."[17]

Fearful his men would not arrive in Mississippi in time to be of use, Lee ensured it would be so by not sending them at all. As events would reveal, his assumptions informing his decision proved almost entirely wrong, from the amount of time it would take re-enforcements to get from east to west—it took Beauregard's men eight days, for instance—to the action being over by month's end to Grant retiring because of the June climate.[18] One might imagine the impact of Pickett's 7,500 additional men, or twice that many including Hood, with Grant pinned against the Big Black River or the outer defenses of Vicksburg. How might Longstreet's sturdy presence have impacted the performance of the fretful Johnston, whom he respected and liked? While only speculative, the possibilities tantalize.

As Seddon levered into motion what re-enforcements he could, Davis tried to shake off his torpor. He was

---

17 Lee to Seddon, 10 May 1863, O.R. XXV, pt. 2, 790.

18 It's worth noting, too, that in September 1863, it took nine days for Longstreet's entire corps to shift from Virginia to Georgia just in time for the battle of Chickamauga.

having difficulty seeing out of his one good eye, and a swollen throat made speaking, eating, and swallowing difficult. The news about a Grant victory at Port Gibson, Mississippi, on May 1 was too much for the president to stand, though. He wrote to state Gov. John Pettus asking for "militia, or persons exempt from military service, who may be temporarily organized to repel the invasion."[19]

"I am organizing all the troops possible and I need arms and ammunition. . ." Pettus replied. "[O]ur arsenal is almost exhausted," he said, but promised, "Our people will fight."[20] Davis pledged four thousand rifles and muskets to arrive in Jackson within three or four days. "I think we shall be able to supply all the forces which you can raise," he said.[21]

Davis did not hear back from Pettus for almost a week. When he did, on May 8, the message could not have been more alarming: "Hour of trial is on us. We look to you for assistance. Let it be speedy."[22]

---

19 Davis to Pettus, 2 May 1863, O.R. LII, Vol. 2, 464.

20 Pettus to Davis, 4 May 1863, O.R. LII, Vol. 2, 464.

21 Davis to Pettus, 4 May 1863, O.R. LII, Vol. 2, 467.

22 Pettus to Davis, 8 May 1863, O.R. LII, Vol. 2, 468.

4

THE HEAD-QUARTERS OF EVERYTHING

NAMED FOR war hero Andrew Jackson, Jackson, Mississippi, was founded in 1821 as a trading post at the intersection of the Natchez Trace and the Pearl River.[1] Its importance as a transportation hub grew over time as major north-south and east-west railroads converged there. That, in turn, transformed Jackson into a major commercial and manufacturing center, driven by increasing demand for the state's number-one crop, cotton. By 1861, Mississippi had become the largest cotton-producing state in the country, and much of it flowed on iron rails through Jackson. The city's relative geographic centrality also made it an ideal location as the state capital. The legislature convened there in a newly completed capitol building for the first time on December 23, 1822, just two days before Christmas.

As Mississippi's capital, Jackson was home to a number of state functions. A traveler in 1859 documented the state arsenal, a penitentiary, a "lunatic asylum," an "Institution of the Blind" and "the Deaf and Dumb Institute," and educational institutions and primary departments "of the

---

1 Timothy B. Smith, "Jackson: The Capital and the Civil War," *Mississippi History Now*, http://mshistorynow.mdah.state.ms.us/articles/337/jackson-the-capital-city-and-the-civil-war (accessed 27 December 2020).

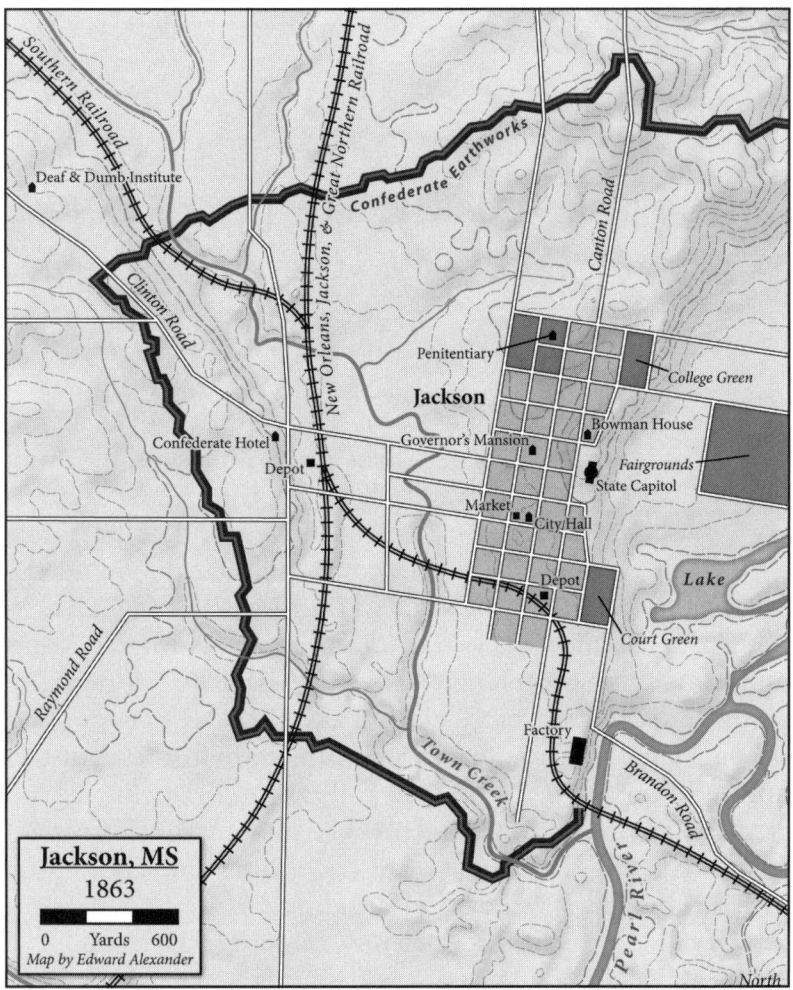

JACKSON, MS

Prior to Grant's arrival, Jackson had remained largely undisturbed during the war because it sat safely in the state's interior, allowing it to maintain its key role as a manufacturing and transportation hub. As Mississippi's capital, Jackson housed a number of state institutions, such as the capitol, the state penitentiary, and the deaf and dumb institute. The state insane asylum was north of town (off the map) along the Canton Road. A thin line of hasty fortifications ringed the city on the eve of battle, anchored at each end on the banks of the Pearl River.

Edward Alexander

The Head-Quarters of Everything | 31

"The 'State House' is built partly of limestone of an inferior character and partly of brick, which gives the appearance of being an older edifice than it really is," wrote an 1859 traveler. "At a distance, however, it presents a rather grand exhibition of architecture." It looked unchanged by the time an artist sketched it for *Scribner's* in 1874.

Scribner's

---

first class."[2] The state capitol presented "a rather grand exhibition of architecture" and the executive mansion "the handsomest abode to be seen in the Southern country." State fairgrounds sat on the east edge of the city.

At the heart of town, City Hall housed municipal functions as well as the United States Circuit Court and the Masonic and Odd Fellows Halls. The city boasted three hotels—the Bowman House, "a most capital hotel"; the Dixon House, "not of an inferior order . . . yet more

---

2   This and the following descriptions from George Steuckrath, "Jackson, Mississippi," *De Bow's Review and Industrial Resources, Statistics, etc.*, J. D. B. De Bow, ed., Vol. 26:4 (New Orleans: 1859), 466-8.

The Bowman House hotel in Jackson, Mississippi—"one of the handsomest and best known hotels in the South before the Civil War"—as it appeared in 1863.

Courtesy of the Archives and Records Services Division, Mississippi Department of Archives and History

private in its character"; and the Confederate Hotel, a large frame building near the railroad depot—as well as several smaller boarding houses.[3] Baptist, Catholic, Christian, Episcopal, Methodist, and Presbyterian congregations all had their own churches, and the Jewish community had a congregation, as well. "The attendance is always large," noted the traveler, "which gives assurance that Jackson is a place of high moral character."

Three newspapers vied for the town's readership: *Eagle of the South*, *Mississippi Baptist*, and the oldest paper in the state, *The Mississippian*—"one of the most

---

3 Description of the Confederate Hotel comes from William T. Sherman, *Memoirs of General W. T. Sherman* (New York: Library of America, 1990), 347.

virulent Secession sheets in the whole South," a New York journalist once said.[4]

Ironically, a town named for a man who once declared "Our Federal Union—It Must be Preserved" became the site of Mississippi's secession vote on January 9, 1861. "Our position is thoroughly identified with the institution of slavery—the greatest material interest of the world," the conventioneers declared.[5] At the time, fifty-five percent of the state's 790,000 people were enslaved. Hinds County, where Jackson was located, had the state's highest slave-to-master ratio in Mississippi—and ninth-highest in the south—with 1,421 white households holding 22,363 people in bondage.[6] Statewide, nearly half of all white families were slaveowners.

Jefferson Davis—ironically albeit unintentionally so—evoked the evil of slavery when he made his post-Christmas visit to Jackson in 1862. Speaking to the legislature, but really to the broader Southern public, Davis attempted to rally support for the Confederate government, the Conscription Act and its exemptions for the wealthy, and the overall war effort. The alternative, he warned, was subjugation. "Will you be slaves, or will you be independent?" he asked. Apparently slavery, which Mississippi had declared "the greatest material interest of

---

[4] Junius Henri Browne, *Four years in Secessia: Adventures Within and Beyond the Union Lines, Embracing a Great Variety of Facts, Incidents, and Romances of the War* (Hartford: O. D. Case and Company, 1865), 249.

[5] "A Declaration of the Immediate Causes which Induce and Justify the Secession of the State of Mississippi from the Federal Union," 9 January 1861, Mississippi Secession Convention. https://avalon.law.yale.edu/19th_century/csa_missec.asp (accessed 7 January 2021).

[6] Brian Johnson, "When Jackson Burned," *Jackson Free Press*, 17 May 2006. https://www.jacksonfreepress.com/news/2006/may/17/johnson-when-jackson-burned/ (accessed 3 March 2021).

Mississippi's "splendid soil grows cotton superbly," said one travel writer, writing about the backbone of the state's economy. He noted "many an empire has been founded upon a less extent of territory...."

Scribner's

---

the world," was *not* so great if white Mississippians were going to be the slaves.[7]

Jackson, at the time, had a population of just under 3,200 people—and by May 5, 1863, most of that population was in "great excitement" over the news that Grant had landed a sizable force on the east bank of the Mississippi River. "At the street corners were knots of excited men, discussing the prospects of the future with more feeling than logic . . ." wrote a correspondent for the *New York Tribune*, Junius Henri Browne. "[I]t was evident they were at a loss what to do. . . ."[8]

---

7   Davis, speech to Mississippi legislature.

8   Browne's account here and in the paragraphs that follow come from Browne, 248-9.

BRIG. GEN. JOHN ADAMS
John Adams graduated from the vaunted West Point Class of 1846. Classmates included Thomas "Stonewall" Jackson, George B. McClellan, Darius Couch, Dabney Maury, Cadmus Wilcox, and George Pickett.

Tennessee State Library and Archives

There was much to be done, though. "Jackson was then the headquarters of everything military and civil in this department, outside of Vicksburg," explained a member of the 14th Mississippi, identified in his postwar recollection as "W" from Yazoo City.

The regiment, which had been organized in Jackson in October 1861, had recently returned there for garrison duty under Brig. Gen. John Adams, commander of Mississippi's Fourth Military District. It had been an easy hometown assignment—until suddenly it wasn't. "Grant was uncoiling his ponderous army, and slowly enveloping Vicksburg in its fatal folds," said "W." Everyone seemed nervous. "Army teamsters swore at their mules, and their wagons sunk to the hubs in the muddy streets," "W" added. "Quartermasters, commissaries, paymasters, and a hoard of gamblers with bogus passes in their pockets, thronged the sidewalks."[9]

---

9 "W," "The Doomed City: A Reminiscence of Jackson, Mississippi," *The* (Jackson) *Clarion*, 13 October 1881. Reprinted at https://mississippiconfederates.wordpress.com/2015/03/30/the-doomed-city-a-reminiscence-of-jackson-mississippi/. (accessed 15 March 2021).

MISSISSIPPI GOVERNOR JOHN JONES PETTUS
Biographer Robert Dubay described Governor and "Mississippi fire-eater" John Jones Pettus as a paradox: "On certain occasions he displayed an uncommon cautiousness, prudence, and foresight not always found in a man of his ideological temperament. At other times, Pettus was naïve, unprepared, unimaginative, and wholly impractical."

Mississippi Department of Archives and History

Mayor Charles H. Manship tried to allay tensions by posting handbills throughout the capital proclaiming "not the least cause for alarm" and, according to Browne, "calling the people of Mississippi to arms, to repel the barbarous invader from the soil he polluted with his footsteps, and all that sort of stereotyped rant and braggadocio for which the South has ever been famous."

"The bellicose poster. . . did not seem to have the desired effect," Browne noted wryly, adding, "The Mayor was himself a fugitive before the paste on his defiant *pronunciamiento* was fairly dry." Manship wasn't the only person on the run, either. "If the citizens were flying to arms, they must have concealed [their arms] somewhere in the country, and have been making haste in that direction to recover them," Browne deadpanned. "They were certainly leaving town by all possible routes, and by every obtainable means of conveyance."

It was, he thought, a panic of "the most decided kind." "We saw a number of vehicles of various kinds loaded with household furniture, and men, women, children, and black servants, all greatly excited, moving rapidly out of town," Browne observed. "[N]egroes . . . enjoyed the quandary of their masters and mistresses."

Townsfolk also crammed the train station on the west edge of the city. "The depot was crowded with crushing and elbowing human beings, swaying to and fro—baggage being thrown hither and thither—horses wild with fright, and negroes with confusion," wrote temporary resident Mary Ann Loughborough; "and so we ourselves in a car amid the living stream that flowed and surged along—seeking the Mobile cars—seeking the Vicksburg cars—seeking anything to bear them away from the threatened and fast depopulating town." Yet even as the train chugged westward, she wondered, "[I]s there any place where one is perfectly safe in these troubled times?"[10]

On May 3, following news of the Federal victory at Port Gibson, Governor Pettus directed an ersatz defense of Jackson by ordering the construction of earthworks around the city. The work was done, at first, by enslaved people "borrowed" by the government from local residents. Citizens generally complied, but a few first asked for assurances the government would pay for the services of their slaves.[11] As it was, Pettus had authority to impress enslaved labor "for public safety," a power granted to him the previous December by the state legislature.[12]

"Jackson was to be defended!!" exclaimed Loughborough, "which I doubted"—her pessimism immediately offsetting her exclamation points.[13]

---

10 Mary Ann Loughborough, *My Cave Life in Vicksburg, with Letters if Trial and Travel* (New York: A. Appleton & Co., 1864), 28, 29.

11 Robert W. Dubay, *John Jones Pettus, Mississippi Fire-Eater: His Life and Times, 1813-1867* (Jackson, MS: University Press of Mississippi, 1975), 169-70.

12 Dubay, 154-5.

13 Loughborough, 26.

The Pearl River noodled from northeast to southwest, and Jackson sat on the outside of one of the noodle bends. The river's overall course, though, allowed Confederates to encase the capital in a ring of entrenchments that anchored on the river north and south of the city. The impressed laborers bent their backs to the work, digging and shoveling and hauling, powered by government-issued rations.

The project didn't proceed at a fast-enough pace, though, so white volunteers joined in the effort while others volunteered to serve in the rifle-pits in defense of the city, bolstering Adams's small garrison of men.[14] "Jackson presents a lively appearance," said *The Mississippian*.[15] But appearances, as the old adage warns, were deceiving: Pettus made arrangements to move the state government to Enterprise, some 100 miles to the east.[16]

"Every tumult in the town caused us to fly to the doors and windows, fearing a surprise at any time," recalled Loughborough, who lived across the street from one of the newly constructed artillery emplacements. There was, she said, "a panic and dismay."[17]

---

14 Edwin C. Bearss, *The Campaign for Vicksburg*, Vol 2: *Grant Strikes a Fatal Blow,* (El Dorado Hills, CA: Savas Beatie, 2021), 530-1.

15 Quoted in the *Montgomery* (AL) *Daily Mail,* 15 May 1863, 2.

16 Bearss, 527, n33.

17 Loughborough, 27-8.

5

The Decision to Move on Jackson

As the work progressed on Jackson's defenses, Grant honed in, his corps moving along parallel roads in supporting distance of one another the way a three-legged stool will twist in an arc as it pivots from one leg to the next: John McClernand's XIII Corps, James McPherson's XVII Corps, and, arriving last on the Mississippi's east bank, William Sherman's XV Corps—somewhere in the neighborhood of 40,000 men present for duty.[1] Grant always kept a strong screen between his corps and Vicksburg to the west, from where Pemberton's forces might suddenly materialize at any moment. The screen also made it difficult for Pemberton to discern Grant's exact intentions or movements because Federals seemed to be everywhere at once.

"My scouts . . . saw cavalry on the Jackson road," reported Col. Thomas Scott of the 12th Louisiana on the afternoon of May 11. "Citizens and negroes report a heavy force of cavalry, artillery, and infantry. . . . I myself heard drums northeast of this place. . . ."[2] Maj. Gen. Carter Stevenson, meanwhile, reported that a prisoner claimed 40,000 Federals were converging on Jackson—"the whole

---

1 Please see the extended note at the end of this chapter for more about Grant's numbers.

2 Scott to Crowder, 11 May 1863, O.R. XXIV, Pt. 3, 856-7.

MAJ. GENS. JAMES MCPHERSON AND WILLIAM T. SHERMAN

"There was no 'fear' in 'McPherson,'" says historian Kris White, explaining the correct pronunciation of James McPherson's surname. *Library of Congress*

William T. Sherman initially believed "this whole plan of attack on Vicksburg will fail must fail, and the fault will be on us all of course." However, Grant's continuing success made him a true believer. *Library of Congress*

---

army in motion," Stevenson said. But, he realized, the prisoner might have been a plant and so did not know whether to believe him. "I do not know the circumstances under which he was taken," Stevenson admitted. "He may have been sent on."[3] Complicating the picture even further, rumors came in that Federals were advancing from Corinth in the north, with more descending from as far away as Memphis.

The fog of war hung heavy over west-central Mississippi.

3 Stevenson to Memminger, 11 May 1863, Pt. 3, 857.

Pemberton told subordinates in the field to look for any possible opening, "in which case you must be prepared to attack them in rear and on flank."[4]

One of those subordinates was Brig. Gen. John Gregg, whose 3,300-man brigade of Texans and Tennesseans had been recalled north from its posting near Port Hudson, Louisiana. Their march north had been "long and tiresome . . ." recalled Pvt. W. J. Davidson of the 41st Tennessee, "with loads heavy enough to break down a mule." The men trudged along hot, dusty lanes, panting with heat and thirst, their feet blistering, their legs swelling. "[O]ur rations gave out, and the heat and dust became almost insufferable," he wrote.[5] By the time they arrived in Jackson on May 9, a newspaper correspondent said Gregg's men "looked way-worn and dusty, and some had thrown away their shoes." Their pride kicked in as they entered town, though: "[T]hey closed ranks, straightened up, and trod with elastie step, and proud, defiant faces."[6]

On May 12, Gregg's brigade found itself tussling with Grant's army just outside the town of Raymond, Mississippi, fifteen miles southwest of Jackson. An early Confederate advantage evaporated, and by midafternoon, Federals routed Gregg from the field. Gregg's bedraggled men retreated back to the capital for safety.

Grant pursued.

---

4 Pemberton to Gregg, 11 May 1863, O.R. XXIV, Pt. 3, 856. Similar orders went to John Bowen and William Loring, see pp. 854, 856.

5 W. J. Davidson, "Diary of Private W. J. Davidson, Company C, Forty-First Tennessee Regiment," *Annals of the Army of Tennessee and early western history*, (Nashville, TN: A. D. Haynes, 1878), 166-167.

6 Special Correspondent, "Letter from Jackson, May 10th," *Mobile Daily Advertiser and Register*, 15 May 1863, 1.

MAJ. GEN. JOHN MCCLERNAND
John McClernand's corps would not be involved in the battle of Jackson because it was guarding Grant's western flank. However, McClernand would perform well over the course of the campaign. His worst enemy would be himself.

Library of Congress

"I determined to move rapidly upon Jackson," Grant later explained, "and capture and destroy that place and the railroads leading to and from it before turning toward Vicksburg."[7]

His decision proved one of his most important improvisations of the campaign.

"All the enemy's supplies of men and stores would come by that point [Jackson]," Grant later explained.[8] While he tasked McPherson with targeting the railroad for that very reason, just severing the line might not be enough. The affair at Raymond had raised the possibility of a more substantial Confederate threat to the Federal army's right flank and rear than Grant had originally credited. As early as the 6th, he'd heard that Confederate reinforcements were on their way, and as Gregg's presence at Raymond demonstrated, those Southern forces had begun to

---

7   John Russell Young, *Around the World with General Grant*, Vol. II (New York: The American News Company, 1879), 621.

8   Ulysses S. Grant, "The Personal Memoirs of Ulysses S. Grant," *Memoirs and Selected Letters,* Mary Drake and William S. McFeely, eds. (New York: Library of America, 1990), 332, hereafter cited as "*Memoirs*."

arrive. Were they to mass in Jackson while Pemberton still threatened from Vicksburg, Grant might find himself attacked from both sides. A move toward Jackson, then Vicksburg, would allow Grant to deliver a one-two blow against the fragmented Confederate forces in detail before they could unite.

A move toward Jackson, though, would also uncover Grant's line of communication and supply. "So I finally decided to have none—to cut loose altogether from my base . . ." he concluded. He determined to "move swiftly toward Jackson, destroy or drive any force in that direction and then turn upon Pemberton."[9] One of the myths of Grant's campaign is that, as his army marched through Mississippi, it lived off the land a la Sherman during the 1864 March to the Sea. Until this decisive moment, though, Grant actually benefited from an effective supply line overseen by the capable Maj. Gen. Frank Blair; only now did he opt to sever it in favor of greater maneuverability.

Once Grant determined to target the capital, his three-legged stool swiveled into counter-clockwise motion. Sherman, as the army's reserve, swung up into position as the new right wing of the army; McPherson, formerly the army's right wing, swung north to become the left wing; and McClernand, formerly the army's left wing, swung westward into a position that would continue to block any advance by Pemberton. "The execution of this movement will pass the flank and rear of our force in the face of the enemy (close by) . . ." McClernand told his division commanders, "and will require great vigilance and promptitude."[10]

---

9 Grant, *Memoirs*, 332. Grant wrote this hokum purely in hindsight, though.

10 McClernand to Hovey, Osterhaus, and Carr, 13 May 1863, O.R. XXIV, Pt. 3, 306.

MAJ. GEN. FRANCIS PRESTON BLAIR, JR. Frank Preston Blair's father was a powerful figure in Republican politics, and Preston's brother, Montgomery, was Lincoln's postmaster general. Preston's immediate superior, Sherman, distrusted "mere politicians who come to fight not for the real glory & success of the nation, but for their own individual aggrandizement," but on his own merits, Blair would eventually rise to corps command under Sherman.

Library of Congress

McPherson's first stop: Clinton, to sever the railroad. From there, Grant said, "Move at early dawn upon Jackson." He added, "Sherman will move at the same hour by the direct Raymond and Jackson road."[11] The prescribed route would bring McPherson to the city from the northwest, Sherman from the southwest along the same road Gregg had taken in retreat.

McPherson's corps arrived in Clinton by 3:00 p.m. on May 13, unmolested but in time to watch a train pass through—"the last that will ever be run by Confederates," one infantryman said. Soldiers set about destroying tracks until after dark. "'Cotton is king,'" the infantryman later wrote, "and finding a good deal here, we have made our beds of it."[12]

---

11 Grant to McPherson, 13 May 1863, O.R. XXIV, Pt. 3, 307.

12 Osborn H. Oldroyd, *A Soldier's Story of the Siege of Vicksburg* (Springfield, IL: H. W. Rokker, 1885), 20.

THE DECISION TO MOVE ON JACKSON | 45

A NOTE ABOUT GRANT'S NUMBERS

Federal numbers for the overland campaign in Mississippi are surprisingly slippery for a number of reasons. My thanks to Timothy B. Smith and Dave Powell for pushing me to really dig on this. I had an especially good exchange with Dave, based on O.R. XXIV, Pt. 3, 249, which lists an aggregate present (AP) of 53,596 at the end of April 1863. As Dave explains, "AP has value, since it represents Grant's mouths to feed, not just trigger pullers." However, he adds, present for duty (PFD) numbers are the ones most commonly used as combat figures. Here's a breakdown:

McClernand's XIII Corps: 19,249 PFD or 19,767 AP. The return actually lists 1,279 officers and 21,411 men PFD or 26,419 AP, but the 13th Division and 2nd Cav division were both at Helena, Arkansas, west of the river, consisting of 3,441 PFD or 6,652 AP. This suggests also that virtually all of the corps' aggregate strength remained west of the river.

Sherman's XV Corps: 17,053 PFD or 20,419 AP

McPherson's XVII Corps: 15,848 PFD or 17,482 AP

TOTALS: 53,139 PFD or 57,668 AP

"But," Dave points out, "that return also then lists the 'Grand total operating against Vicksburg' as only 47,212 officers and men PFD or 53,596 AP. So which other formations is Grant not counting? Clearly not the Helena garrison, but also at least 6,000 other troops (PFD) or 4,000 others troops (AP)—and isn't it also interesting that those numbers don't line up?" (Benjamin Grierson's 1,700 troopers moving on a raid through the Mississippi interior don't seem to be in Grant's tally, for instance.)

Tim Smith suggested the same thing. "I wonder if the 47,000 PFD is still way high, depending on when you're talking about," he suggested. He pointed out that only two of the three divi-sions in each of the XV and XVII Corps crossed initially. "Grant moved inland with only the XIII Corps and Logan's division and later Quinby's (Sanborn's) division of the XVII Corps," Tim ex-plains, "augmented a few days later by Sherman's two XV Corps divisions, later of course aug-mented by the arriving other brigades and divisions of those corps"—which don't arrive until after the battle of Jackson.

So, that gives us:

McClernand's XIII Corps: 19,249 PFD

Sherman's XV Corps: 17,053 PFD – 5,917 men from the Second Division = 11,136 PFD

McPherson's XVII Corps: 15,848 PFD – 4,203 men from the Sixth Division = 11,645 PFD

TOTAL: 42,030

Even that number began to dwindle as Grant moved inland. By mid-May, battle casualties, detachments, and straggling would have brought Grant's effective numbers down below 40,000 officers and men. "Troops have a way of melting away when you start counting bayonets in ranks," Dave says.

Most modern scholars have avoided providing a specific number at this juncture of the cam-paign. Donald Miller, though, places the number on May 9 at "around forty-one thousand" Donald L. Miller, *Vicksburg: Grant's Campaign that Broke the Confederacy* [New York: Simon & Schuster, 2019], 383). Parker Hills places the number on that day at "approximately thirty-five thousand men" (J. Parker Hills, "Roads to Raymond," *The Vicksburg Campaign, March 29–May 18, 1863*, Steven E. Woodworth and Charles D. Grear, eds. [Carbondale, IL: Southern Illinois University Press, 2013], 79).

Early historian Stephen Dill Lee, chair of the Vicksburg Park Commission and onetime participant in the campaign, put Grant's number at an impressively specific 41,367 (Stephen Dill Lee, "The Campaign of Vicksburg, Mississippi, in 1863," *Publications of the Mississippi Historical Society*, Vol. III, Franklin L. Riley, ed. [Oxford, MS: Mississippi Historical Society, 1901], 30).

The fluid number of on-hand troops illustrates a vital practical point. As historian Michael Ballard pointed out, "Grant's ability to get more troops without weakening other fronts, along with the cooperation he had from the navy, contrasted sharply with Pemberton's options" (Michael B. Ballard, *Vicksburg: The Campaign that Opened the Mississippi* [Chapel Hill, NC: UNC Press, 2004], 253).

Finally, it's worth nothing, on May 9, Grant and his subordinates were thinking of their force in terms of "50,000 men." For examples, see Grant's letter from Rocky Springs, MS, to Col. W. S. Hillyer, 9 May 1863 (*The Papers of Ulysses S. Grant, Volume 8: April 1–July 6, 1863*, John Y. Simon, ed. [Carbondale, IL: Southern Illinois University Press, 1979], 186) and Sherman's let-ter from Hankinson's Ferry, MS, to Grant, 9 May 1863 (OR XIV, Pt. 3, 285). It's interesting to speculate on the psychological effect this inflated number may have had on Grant's strategic and tactical thinking.

TO CLINTON AND JACKSON

After the battle of Raymond on May 12, Grant faced a crossroads: on to Vicksburg directly or up to Jackson to flush out the growing threat posed by Joe Johnston?

Chris Mackowski

6

A Show of Saving the City

WHEN GREGG fell back to Jackson, he did his best to raise the alarm. "The enemy are advancing from Raymond in force," he reported to Pemberton. The problem was that he didn't know if Grant was advancing northeast toward Jackson or northwest toward Edwards Station and a crossing of the Big Black River—the route to Vicksburg. The screen provided by Sherman's 4th Iowa Cavalry proved too opaque to see through. The best Gregg could do was "retire before them until further re-enforcements or other orders."[1]

"You must not attack the enemy in superior force," Pemberton replied, "but fall back, if necessary, to Jackson, and occupy entrenchments."[2] After the battle of Raymond, Pemberton did not want Gregg provoking a rematch that would further deplete his forces. Jackson didn't boast fortress-like fortifications, but Pemberton believed the entrenchments were strong enough to hold back any Federal attempt to sweep into the city. Along with Gregg's brigade, and Adams's scant garrison, the city's defenders included six companies of the 3rd Kentucky Mounted Infantry and one brigade—about 1,200 men—under Brig. Gen. W. H. T. Walker, recently arrived from Savannah,

---

1   Gregg to Pemberton, O.R. XXIV, Pt. 3, 873.

2   Pemberton to Gregg, O.R. XXIV, Pt. 3, 873.

BRIG. GEN.
W. H. T. WALKER
William Henry Talbot Walker earned the nickname "Shot Pouch" because he attracted so much lead from multiple woundings during his service in the war with Mexico.

Generals in Gray

Georgia, as part of the reinforcements Beauregard had sent at Davis's urging. Nicknamed "Shot-Pouch" because of his propensity for attracting enemy fire, Walker was "a fierce and very warlike fire-eater" whose military service dated back to the Mexican-American War; this would be his first time under fire since 1847.[3]

Jackson was also packed with supplies, so any force holding the city could do so for days. With any luck, besieged Confederates might hold Grant's attention long enough to let Pemberton approach with a force from the rear and catch Grant in a vise.

Not that Gregg, Walker, and Adams would have to hold the position alone. As Davis had promised, other reinforcements were imminent: Brig. Gen. States Rights Gist's brigade from Beauregard's army in Charleston. "I expect to reach Jackson Thursday morning," Gist wired on Tuesday, May 12. "General Beauregard desires that we be kept together."[4] The first elements of Gist's force—the

---

3 Fremantle, 117; Russell K. Brown, *To the Manner Born: The Life of General William H. T. Walker* (Macon, GA: Mercer University Press, 2005), 151.

4 Gist to Pemberton, O.R. XXIV, Pt. 3, 862.

BRIG. GEN. STATES RIGHTS GIST
Of States Rights Gist, "some wag has remarked that with a name like that, he had to fight for the Confederacy!" wrote historian Ed Bearss.

Emerging Civil War

24th South Carolina, the 46th Georgia, and the 8th Georgia Battalion, all under the command of Col. Peyton Colquitt—began to arrive sometime during the night of the 13th.

In addition, Brig. Gen. Samuel Maxey's brigade was expected to arrive from Port Hudson, and the reinforcements from Bragg's army in Tennessee, Ector's and McNair's brigades, were also on the way. "The prospect in Mississippi grows more encouraging from moment to moment," wrote a newspaper correspondent. "Heavy trains from Georgia, and other positions of the Confederacy east of Jackson, are hourly pouring in, loaded with reinforcements."[5]

The new arrivals gave the newspaperman something to wonder about, though. "As the cars stop at the depot, the men stroll off, and in the course of an hour or two return, many of them more than half [drunk]," he wrote. "Where they procure the liquor is a question, the solution of which would infinitely delight many of the residents of Jackson, your correspondent included; but it is almost incredible that private soldiers, with $11 a month, can

---

5 Special Correspondent, "Letter from Jackson, May 10th."

BRIG. GEN. JOHN GREGG
In 1863, Brig. Gen. John Gregg commanded troops in several western campaigns but would find his most renown—and his death—commanding Hood's Texas Brigade for the Army of Northern Virginia in 1864.

Library of Congress

obtain enough bad whiskey 'to make the drunk come,' when the article is retailed at $15 a bottle, and hard to get at that."[6]

With Pemberton ensconced with the Vicksburg defenders, Gregg was senior man on the field. Pemberton tried to advise him from afar. "All the force now there and arriving will be kept for the defense of that place for the present," Pemberton told him. However, if Grant moved toward Edwards Station instead of Jackson, Pemberton expected the forces in Jackson to look for an opening: "[Y]ou will advance on his flank and rear, taking care not to get into a position to be cut off."[7]

Not until the late evening of May 13 did Grant's shift toward the capital finally become apparent. "From every source, both black and white, I learn that the enemy are moving on Jackson," reported one subordinate to Pemberton. "I think there can be no doubt of this."[8] By that point, though, Pemberton had no reliable way to pass

---

6   Ibid.

7   Pemberton to Gregg, O.R. XXIV, Pt. 3, 873.

8   Loring to Pemberton, O.R. XXIV, Pt. 3, 875.

information on to Johnston. Their last communication had connected sometime that afternoon when Johnston stopped at Lake Station, some fifty miles east of Jackson. In the dispatch, Pemberton incorrectly predicted a Federal advance on Edwards Station.

Things appeared no clearer for Johnston when he arrived at Jackson a few hours after that, "exhausted by an uninterrupted journey of four days, taken from a sick-room," he claimed.[9] He made his headquarters at the Bowman House, a five-story hotel on the corner of State and Amite streets across from the state capitol. Built in 1857, the Bowman was called "one of the handsomest and best known hotels in the South."[10] Johnston summoned Gregg for a status report. Unfortunately, Gregg—exhausted after his fight at Raymond the previous day and scrambling to organize the defense of the city—possessed an incomplete picture about Grant's movements and incorrect information about Pemberton's location. According to Gregg, Sherman was astride the railroad ten miles west of Jackson, with Pemberton at Edwards Station four miles beyond that. He would have been shocked to know it was McPherson, not Sherman, who was approaching—yet undetected—from the northwest.

Johnston also took time to learn about the fortifications around the city, although no record exists that he did any sort of personal inspection. If he had, he certainly would have been underwhelmed. One observer later described the works as "a mild trench, which was dignified by the name of 'the fortifications of Jackson.'"[11] The best that could be said of them was that some seventeen artillery

---

9   Joseph E. Johnston, "Jefferson Davis and the Mississippi Campaign," *Battles & Leaders of the Civil War*, vol. 3, Robert Underwood Johnson, ed. (New York: The Century Co., 1883), 479. Hereafter cited as "*B&L*."

10 Smith, "Jackson."

11 Fremantle, 105.

pieces bolstered the ring around the city, supplemented by the field batteries.

And thus Johnston's pessimistic message to Richmond: "I arrived this evening, finding the enemy's force between this place and General Pemberton, cutting off the communication. I am too late."[12]

Historian Steven Woodworth has identified this as the moment of decision for the Gibraltar of the Confederacy. "[I]t was not too late to save Vicksburg—not quite," he writes, "but with that attitude Johnston could certainly help to make it so over the course of the next few days. Whether it was too late to save Jackson was another story."[13]

Johnston made a show of trying to save the city. At 8:40 p.m., he sent a message to Pemberton suggesting action. He pointed to the Federal force astride the railroad between them, misidentifying it (thanks to Gregg) as Sherman, not McPherson. "It is important to re-establish communications, that you may be re-enforced," Johnston told Pemberton. "If practicable, come on his rear at once. To beat such a detachment, would be of immense value. The troops here would co-ordinate. All the strength you can quickly assemble should be brought. Time is all important."[14]

Then, with that hammer-and-anvil plan in place and additional reinforcements imminent, with time pressing, Johnston made the puzzling decision to abandon Jackson. His show of saving the city was over.

Yet even then, after he began the evacuation of the city, Johnston beckoned to Pemberton to come on. "If prisoners tell the truth, the forces at Jackson must be half

12 Johnston to Seddon, 13 May 1863, O.R. XXIV, Pt. 1, 215.

13 Steven Woodworth, "The First Capture of Jackson," *The Vicksburg Campaign* (Carbondale, IL: Southern Illinois University Press, 2013), 100.

14 Johnston to Pemberton, 13 May 1863, O.R. XXIV, Pt. 3, 870.

MAJ. SAMUEL H. LOCKETT
A native of Alabama, born in Virginia, Samuel Lockett graduated second in the West Point Class of 1859.

Battles and Leaders

of Grant's army," he wrote on the morning of May 14. "It would decide the campaign to beat it, which can be done only by concentrating. . . ."[15]

Davis had ordered Pemberton to defend Vicksburg; Johnston had ordered Pemberton to take the offensive. The orders, said Pemberton's chief engineer, Samuel H. Lockett, "were very conflicting in their tenor." Pemberton felt caught between the rock of Gibraltar and a hard place. The central tension between Davis and Johnston over strategy along the Mississippi, which had gone unresolved between them for months and had festered in Johnston's craw like a canker, finally proved untenable.

According to Lockett, Pemberton "then made the capital mistake of trying to harmonize instructions from his superiors diametrically opposed to each other, and at the same time to bring them into accord with his own judgment, which was adverse to the plans of both."[16]

What followed over the next few days between Pemberton and Johnston could be called a comedy of

---

15 Johnston to Pemberton, 14 May 1863, O.R. XXIV, Pt. 3, 877.

16 S. H. Lockett, "The Defense of Vicksburg," *Battles & Leaders of the Civil War*, vol. 3, Robert Underwood Johnson, ed. (New York: The Century Co., 1883), 487.

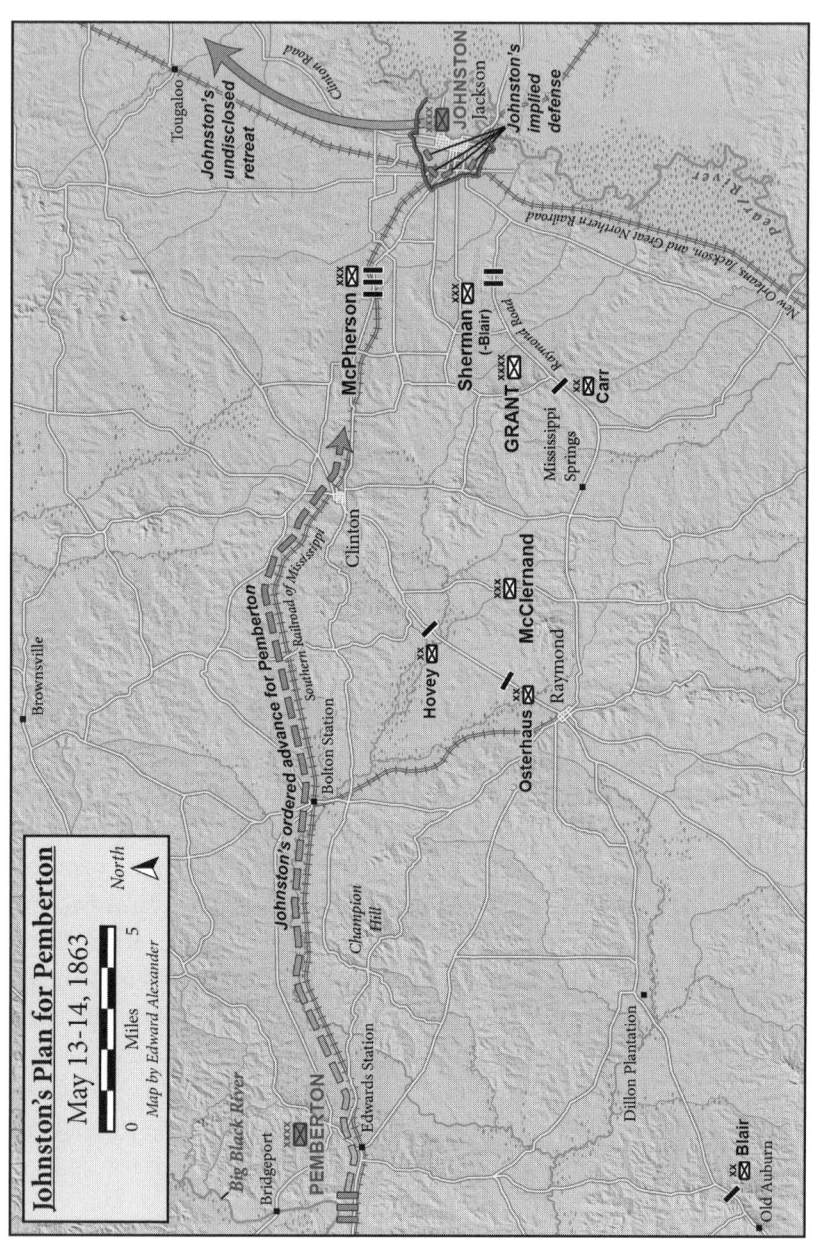

JOHNSTON'S PLAN FOR PEMBERTON

Believing Sherman (not McPherson) was astride the railroad to the west of Jackson, Joe Johnston urged John Pemberton to move in on the Federals from behind. In written orders late on May 13 and early on May 14, Johnston led Pemberton to believe that the two Confederate forces would coordinate efforts in an attempt to beat the Federal detachment. Despite his comments about concentrating, Johnston instead fled Jackson—a move he did not disclose to Pemberton even as he urged Pemberton onward.

Edward Alexander

---

errors if it hadn't led to the loss of so many lives and the eventual fall of Vicksburg. "[C]onfusion and consequent disasters resulted, which might have been avoided. . ." Davis later lamented, from miles away and years distant, through the lens of hindsight.[17]

With a portion of his army left behind to man the Hill City's defenses, Pemberton reluctantly sallied forth with 22,000 men to make a strike at Grant's supply lines, then changed direction, then eventually blundered into Grant at Champion Hill on May 16, all in response to conflicting and outright disingenuous messages from Johnston. "Pemberton moved out from Edward's depot in obedience to a dispatch from General Johnston, ordering him to attack in the rear a force which he supposed General Johnston was going to engage in front," Lockett recalled. "Instead of this, he encountered Grant's victorious army returning, exultant and eager for more prizes, from the capture of Jackson."[18]

All the while, messages between Johnston and Pemberton crisscrossed in transit because of their insecure communication line, confusing matters further.

---

17 Johnston, on pg. 479 in his *B&L* article, quotes Davis from volume two of *Rise and Fall of the Confederate Government*, 404-5.

18 Lockett, 487.

As a result of the lag, Johnston got his hackles up because he came to the mistaken impression at one point that Pemberton was willfully disobeying him. Historian John R. Lundberg suggests Johnston then spun his response, "apparently intend[ing] his orders on May 15 to emphasize that Pemberton had disobeyed his earlier orders and therefore should bear the blame for the loss of Vicksburg."[19] Confederates had not yet lost the city, yet Johnston was already setting up his fall guy, just as he believed Davis had likewise set up him.

Pemberton did dither at times, but he did also make an honest effort at following his commander's orders and clearing up the confusion. "In directing this move, I do not think you fully comprehend the position that Vicksburg will be left in," he warned at the outset, "but I comply at once with your order."[20] To his staff, the Vicksburg commander offered a more blunt assessment: "Such a movement will be suicidal."[21] So it would nearly prove to be.

And all the while, as Pemberton tried to execute Johnston's mercurially shifting orders, Johnston would be marching away from the Vicksburg army in the opposite direction.

Johnston set his evacuation plan into motion by 3:30 a.m. on May 14. He first ordered the city's vast storehouses of food and supplies loaded onto a wagon train and directed it toward Canton, some twenty-five miles to the northeast. This task fell mostly to Adams's garrison troops, although the 14th Mississippi—which had enjoyed the relative comforts of hometown duty—was detached for duty on what was about to become the front line. The hometown regiment was "rudely awakened from

---

19 Lundberg, 125.

20 Pemberton to Johnston, 14 May 1863, O.R. XXIV, Pt. 3, 877.

21 Pemberton, O.R. XXIV, Pt. 1, 269.

its dream of inglorious ease," recalled "W." "[W]e bade our adieu to Jackson, folded our tents, fell into line, and silently marched away. . . ."[22]

Johnston then ordered Samuel Maxey's 3,000 approaching reinforcements to fall back to Brookhaven, fifty-five miles to the south, where Pemberton might call on him to link up.[23] He also sent a wire to States Rights Gist, closing in from the east with his Charleston reinforcements, and directed him "to assemble the approaching troops at a point 40 or 50 miles from Jackson." Johnston hoped they would be able "to prevent the enemy in Jackson from drawing provisions from the east. . . ."[24] The Federals had not even arrived, yet Johnston spoke as if the city had already been lost.

Had Johnston instead concentrated Maxey's and Gist's reinforcements with Gregg's, Adams's, and Walker's troops already in Jackson, he might have assembled a force of close to 15,000 men—perhaps not enough to stop Grant's force of 44,000 but certainly enough to significantly complicate matters for him, particularly with Pemberton's 22,000-man force converging nearby.[25] Beating Grant would "decide the campaign," Johnston had said, which could only be done by concentrating—so by that same logic, the reverse would also be true: without concentrating, Confederates couldn't beat Grant. Johnston was fulfilling his own prediction.

As he eyed the road out of town, Johnston ordered Gregg and Walker to make a stand and hold out as long as

---

22 W, "The Doomed City."

23 Johnston to Pemberton, 15 May 1863, O.R. XXIV, Pt. 3, 882.

24 Johnston to Pemberton, 14 May 1863, O.R. XXIV, Pt. 3, 877.

25 Johnston made this estimation himself in an article in *Battles & Leaders*, vol. 3, 479.

they could in the hope that Adams could get the supplies far enough away that they'd be out of Federal reach.

Aware that Federals had severed the railroad at Clinton, Gregg expected them to advance from that direction, so he posted Colquitt's demi-brigade to the northwest of the city some three miles out near the farm of local resident O. P. Wright, and he placed a portion of Walker's troops—the 30th Georgia and the 4th Louisiana Infantry Battalion—"within easy supporting distance" behind Colquitt. The Wright home sat atop a ridge with a cleared slope three-quarters of a mile long in the direction of Clinton, with timber in the ravine at the bottom. Infantry deployed along the downslope: the 24th South Carolina, the 46th Georgia, and the newly reassigned 14th Mississippi. Upslope, Capt. James Hoskins's Brookhaven Light Artillery deployed four rifled pieces along the crest of the ridge, unlimbering around the house, a cotton gin, and other outbuildings.[26] A second battery deployed on Colquitt's left. Federals later attested that the Confederate batteries had "a good range across open field."[27]

Gregg then marched his own brigade, now under the command of Col. Robert Farquharson, two-and-a-half miles out the Clinton road and moved them across another open field, knee deep in mud, to position them on Colquitt's right flank.[28] "[W]henever within sight of the enemy," Gregg ordered them, "make such demonstrations as might impress him with the idea that it was our

---

26 John Quincy Adams Campbell, *The Union Must Stand: The Civil War Diary of John Quincy Adams Campbell, 5th Iowa Volunteer Infantry*, Mark Grimsley and D. Todd Miller, eds. (Knoxville, TN: University of Tennessee Press, 2000), 94; Bearss 532.

27 McPherson, O.R. XXIV, Pt. 1, 638.

28 Davidson, 169.

intention to fall upon his left flank."[29] Gregg's combination of position and theatrics made for excellent strategy.

The rest of Walker's men—the 3rd Kentucky Mounted Infantry, Maj. Arthur Shaaff's first battalion of Georgia sharpshooters, and a battery under Capt. Robert Martin—Gregg shifted to the road coming up from Raymond to the southwest, placing them two miles out.

Meanwhile, the evacuation continued. Convicts from the state penitentiary were released, formed into a company, and placed under command of Lt. Alexander Trotter to join the retreating column. "On the march they 'vanished in thin air' like the smoke from Grant's batteries in the distance," said "W."[30]

Rain began to fall sometime in the night, then began to come down in curtains—a fitting metaphor for Johnston's exit.

---

29 Confederate troop dispositions all come from Gregg, O.R. XXIV, Pt. 1, 786.

30 W, "The Doomed City."

7

Life No Charm, Death No Horror

To the northwest of Jackson, Maj. Gen. James Birdseye McPherson began a cautious but steady advance eastward at 5:00 a.m. Thirty-four years old and a graduate of the West Point class of 1853, McPherson was the youngest and least experienced of Grant's corps commanders, but he also enjoyed his commander's favor. Grant spent much time mentoring McPherson and, during the advance through Mississippi, kept close tabs on his movements and dispositions as McPherson grew into his command.

The junior corps commander had successfully captured the railroad at Clinton by 3:00 p.m. on May 13 and interposed himself between Vicksburg and Jackson and any Confederate forces in either that might try to unite. That could have left McPherson's XVII Corps vulnerable to a pincer movement, but McClernand was in easy supporting distance, Sherman was in close coordinated contact, and McPherson was willing to fight, as he'd proven at Raymond on the twelfth.

As he began the move toward Jackson, McPherson sent a note to Sherman to coordinate their arrival in the capital. "General Joe Johnston is in Jackson," McPherson revealed—not knowing Johnston had arrived and already left—"and it is reported they have 20,000 men. I do not think there is that many, though they have collected

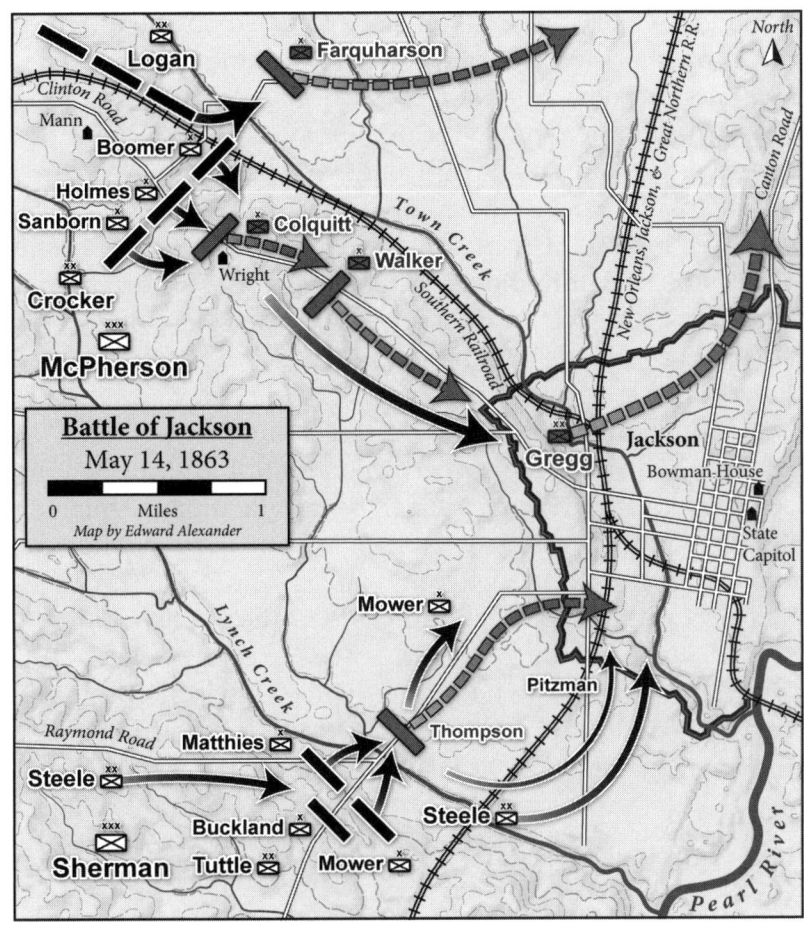

BATTLE OF JACKSON

A two-pronged attack brought Federals toward the state capital from the northwest, under Maj. Gen. James McPherson, and the southwest, under Maj. Gen. William T. Sherman. Confederates scrambled to meet the overwhelming numbers, delaying enough to allow the southern army to evacuate a majority of the supplies stored in the city. Confederates safely escaped even as Federals breached the defenses and pushed into the capital.

Edward Alexander

considerable of a force. They have fortified on the different roads on this side of town, and are forming abatis."[1] That McPherson knew so much about the situation in Jackson revealed another of the Confederates' weaknesses. As historian Ed Bearss put it, "Confederate security measures were conspicuous by their absence. . . ."[2]

After the war, Grant would describe Johnston as "one of the ablest commanders of the south."[3] Whether he felt that way in May 1863 is unclear, but news of Johnston's arrival does not seem to have spooked him. He did nothing to alter the advance of either wing of his army.

McPherson used the Clinton Road as his axis of advance. His corps threw skirmishers out and, under the cover of rain-darkened skies, began "a moist, toilsome march through mud and rain." The mire sucked at cannon axles and wagon wheels, and infantrymen heaved to the work of pushing them free. "What a sight!" an Ohioan exclaimed. "Ambulances creeping along . . . artillery toiling in the deep ruts, while Generals with their aids [sic] and orderlies splashed mud and water in every passing direction. We were all wet to the skin, but plodded

---

[1] McPherson to Sherman, 14 May 1863, O.R. XXIV, Pt. 3, 309. And yes, that considerable of an awkward phrase in the original.

[2] Bearss, 533.

[3] Grant, *Memoirs*, 680. It's worth noting that Grant made this assessment of Johnston twenty years after the war. He also believed that Johnston's strategy of delay, which Johnston had executed on the Virginia Peninsula in the spring of 1862 and which had earned Jefferson Davis's disfavor, "was the best [policy] that one could have been pursued by the whole South" (Memoirs, 632-633). By the time Grant made those assessments, Johnston and Sherman had developed a warm admiration for each other. "Old Joe" and "Uncle Billy" thought highly of each other, which of course helped reinforce their own military prowess, for if their enemy was talented, then they themselves must have been talented, too, to square off with such a worthy opponent. There's no evidence Grant particularly subscribed to this approach, but of all ex-Confederates, Johnston was certainly in the good graces of his former foes even as he was constantly feuding with the ex-Confederate architects of the nascent but growing "Lost Cause" movement.

Federal wagons became so enmired in the heavy rain on May 14 that a pontoon train might have been more useful.

A Soldier's Story of the Siege of Vicksburg

on patiently. . . ."[4] Ahead lay an eventual clash with Colquitt's brigade, centered on the road.[5]

To McPherson's south, his XV Corps counterpart also began to converge on the capital. "We communicated during the night, so as to arrive at Jackson about the same hour," Sherman explained.[6] Gregg, in his retreat from Raymond, had left enough men along the road to keep tabs on the Federal army and slow any advance, so Sherman faced more opposition than McPherson, though the "brave and obstinate enemy" did little to stall him.[7]

The terrain itself proved more the concern. The roads "run along the tops of 'hogback' ridges," wrote Wisconsinite Samuel C. Miles,

> in places barely wide enough for a wagon-track along their crest, with steep timbered sides flanked by deep tangled brush and cane-braked ravines, up and down thickly-timbered and brushy hills and through swampy cane-

---

4   Oldroyd, 20.

5   John D. Stevenson, XXIV, Pt. 1, 717.

6   Sherman, O.R. XXIV, Pt. 1, 753.

7   S. C. Miles, "Capture of Jackson," *The National Tribune,* 27 July 1893, 3.

brake and tangled brush ravines and deep creeks, where the superiority of force is no advantage, as it is impossible to deploy or form line of battle, while the retreating enemy availed himself of every hill and cover to advantageously oppose and harass the advancing column. . . .[8]

"Owing to the nature of the broken and wooded nature of the country, and the known proximity of the enemy, we were required to move slowly with extreme caution," said Col. Lucius F. Hubbard of the 5th Minnesota.[9]

And then, too, there was the rain—the furious rain. "The most drenching rain, which poured down on our men and flooded the roads, made this last march very fatiguing," said Brig. Gen. Charles Matthies.[10] David Reed of the 12th Iowa said the downpour filled "all the low grounds and ditches so that the men were often compelled to wade knee deep in water."[11] Colonel Hubbard groused that "The men were very weary and thoroughly wet":

> having been not only exposed to the storm but required to wade streams and penetrate dense thickets through almost impassable swamps while skirmishing the country through which the column passed. They had also been almost entirely without rations for twenty-four hours. . . . Their heroic endurance of privation and exposure and unexceptionable good conduct in action elicited . . . encomiums of a most flattering character.[12]

---

8   Ibid.

9   Hubbard, O.R. XXIV, Pt. 1, 767.

10 Matthies, O.R. XXIV, Pt. 1, 769.

11 David Wilson Reed, *Campaigns and Battles of the Twelfth Regiment Iowa Veteran Volunteer Infantry* (Evanston, IL: 1903), 118.

12 Hubbard, 768.

Grant, traveling with Sherman, characteristically laid out the situation in simpler terms: "The roads were intolerable," he later grumbled, "and in some places on Sherman's line, where the land was low, they were covered more than a foot deep with water."[13] By daybreak, though, despite the slog, the men felt renewed reason for optimism. "Sharp firing was heard during this march toward our left," Matthies explained. "The men felt cheerful. . . ."[14]

That firing came from McPherson's corps, which came into first contact with Colquitt by 9:00 a.m. Col. Samuel Holmes's brigade of Brig. Gen. Marcellus Crocker's division led the way.[15] "In view of the probability of soon meeting the enemy, a heavy force of skirmishers from the Tenth Missouri was thrown forward and deployed with supports," Holmes recorded. The Missourians found Colquitt's artillery astride the road along a ridge at the Wright farm, with a line of infantry formed in the ravine immediately in its front. Confederate artillery commanded the road, Holmes noted, as well as the "open country of undulating ridges for 1 1/2 miles in the direction of our approach."[16]

Confederate artillery greeted them—the shots heard by Sherman's men to the south—and Holmes responded by consolidating the 10th Missouri skirmishers back into line and deploying the regiment to the right of the road where the 80th Ohio eventually joined them. The 17th Iowa fell in on the road's left side. As the infantry deployed, "The rain-storm which had been falling during the morning now increased in violence," said Maj. Francis C. Deimling of the 10th Missouri, "during which the pieces of the 1st Missouri

---

13 Grant, *Memoirs*, 334.

14 Matthies, 769.

15 Gregg, 786; Holmes, O.R. XXIV, Pt. 1, 775.

16 Holmes, 775.

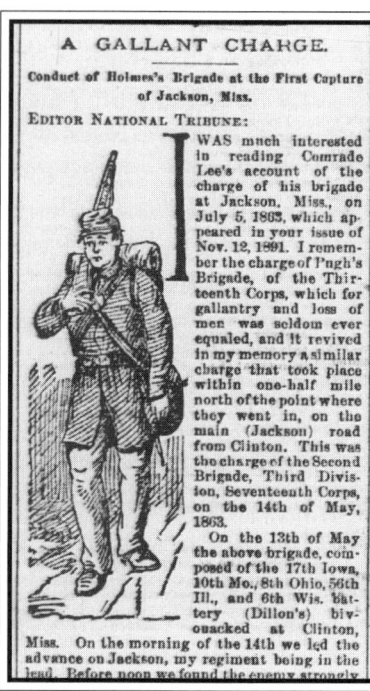

Lt. Harry M. Kenderdine of the 17th Iowa recounted the "Gallant Charge" of Holmes's Brigade more than three decades later in the *National Tribune*, although the soldier in the sketch accompanying the account didn't look all that charged up.

National Tribune

Artillery were placed in position. . . ."[17] The battery unlimbered its four Parrot guns on either side of the W. T. Mann house that sat next to the road and, around 10:00 a.m., returned fire on the Confederates.[18]

As Holmes's brigade deployed, Col. John B. Sanborn's brigade came up on its right and Col. George B. Boomer's brigade came up on its left.[19] With Crocker's division fully deployed, John Logan's division moved into place on Crocker's left, advancing along the railroad they had so recently won, destroying track as they advanced.[20] Logan's deployment effectively blocked Farquharson's Confederate brigade, which had otherwise been perfectly situated on the Federal left for the kind of smashing flank attack Gregg had hoped for. Instead, as the day developed, Farquharson would have to content himself with saving his brigade. Gregg would later put a positive spin on those

---

17 Deimling, O.R. XXIV, Pt. 1, 782; Bearss, 534.

18 McPherson, 638.

19 Holmes, 775.

20 See McPherson to Sherman, 14 May 1863, O.R. XXIV, 309.

BRIG. GEN. MARCELLUS CROCKER

Marcellus Crocker's first name, derived from Latin, translated to "hammer"—a fitting choice for his future exploits on the battlefield, says historian Frank Jastrzembski, who called Crocker "Grant's hammer in the Western Theater." Grant once said of Crocker, "I have never seen but three or four Division commanders his equal and we want his services."

Iowa: Its History and Its Foremost Citizens

events, claiming "the advance of the enemy was very cautious and slow" because Farquharson showed himself in line of battle on the Federal flank.[21]

If the Federals moved with slow caution, that had far more to do with the weather. Troop dispositions took time in the deluge, "the rain coming down in such torrents," said McPherson, "that there was great danger of the ammunition being spoiled if the men opened their cartridge boxes."[22] In all, some ninety minutes passed as the men sloshed into their positions. "During all this time," added Deimling, "the enemy kept up a brisk fire with his artillery with shell and solid shot."[23] The artillery exchange sounded like thunder, which opened from the rainstorm with booms of its own. Infantrymen often confused the two, especially from a distance.

Under the rain of cannonballs, Sanborn discovered "The troops were more exposed to the enemy's artillery fire

21 Gregg, 786.

22 McPherson, 638.

23 Deimling, 782.

Noting the lopsided disparity in forces, a veteran reading McPherson's account of "the formidable dispositions he made to attack the little brigade at Wright's house" found it "almost ludicrous." "McPherson had six brigades arrayed in battle against a little brigade of two battalions, one regiment, and one battery of four guns . . ." the veteran scoffed.

Harper's Weekly

than was at first apprehended. . . ."[24] He moved some of his troops forward to take advantage of cover provided by the ridge occupied by the 1st Missouri Battery but found the area still too hot, "swept by the enemy's fire," particularly with crossfire from the battery on the Confederate left. Sanborn advanced skirmishers from the 59th Indiana to make sure his right flank was safe and, finding it so, ordered the rest of his men forward across the ridge and into the ravine beyond, moving "in perfect line at a run."[25] Sanborn's skirmishers went forward again, topping the next ridge and descending into another ravine beyond where "they were warmly engaged."[26]

Holmes, to Sanborn's left, pushed forward, too. "The whole line advanced in a heavy rain and under a severe

24 Sanborn, O.R. XXIV, Pt. 1, 729.

25 Ibid.

26 McPherson, 638.

LIFE NO CHARM, DEATH NO HORROR | 69

The lithograph *Battle of Jackson, Along the Clinton Road* was produced by Middleton, Strobridge & Co. of Cincinnati, based on a sketch by A. E. Mathews of the 31st Ohio. It depicts the "Gallant charge of the 17th Iowa, 80th Ohio and 10th Missouri, supported by the first and third brigades of the seventh division" against the Confederate position around the Wright house. It's the most widely reproduced image of the battle (although the pool for that distinction is admittedly small).

Library of Congress

---

fire of artillery and skirmishers to within 500 yards of the enemy's main line," he wrote.[27] Along the way, said Col. David B. Hillis of the17th Iowa, they skirmished with southern counterparts "who reluctantly and slowly fell back as I pressed them upon their first line."[28]

Confederates fell back into "a ravine filled with willows," some 150 yards away, where they formed their main line in support of the artillery placed around the Wright house and cotton gin on the ridge behind them.[29]

---

27 Holmes, 775.

28 McPherson, 638; Hillis, O.R. XXIV, Pt. 1, 777.

29 McPherson, 638.

Heavy underbrush separated the opposing combatants, but with Confederate fire so heavy, the skirmishers could not advance any further, and officers recalled them to their regiments.[30] On the lee side of the ridge, Federals hugged the sopping ground to catch their breath and reorganize as artillery shells flew back and forth above them. "[T]he boys were fatigued, their strength almost exhausted, their haversacks entirely empty, and the rain coming down in torrents," said Lt. Harry M. Kenderdine of the 17th Iowa. "Life seemed to have no charms and death no horrors. . . . [F]or a short time, nothing could be heard but the bursting of shell and the whizzing of bullets."[31]

By 2:00 p.m., the rain began to slacken and peeks of blue sky even showed themselves. McPherson, ready to clear the Confederates out once and for all, ordered Crocker's division "to fix bayonets and charge through the ravine all the way to the enemy's batteries, if possible."[32] Hillis, looking to his Iowans on the left end of the line, told his men, "Boys, when I tell you to go down there, I expect you will go."[33]

At the center of the formation, Holmes called his brigade to attention. The men rose to their feet. "Forward, double-quick;" Holmes ordered. "Give them cold steel!"[34] The whole line "swept forward in most

---

30 Hillis, 777; McPherson, 638.

31 H. M. Kenderdine, "A Gallant Charge: The Conduct of Holmes's Brigade at the First Capture of Jackson, Miss," *National Tribune,* 17 March 1892, 4.

32 Sanborn, 729.

33 Addison A. Stuart, "Colonel David Burke Hillis: Second Colonel, Seventeenth Iowan Infantry," *Iowan Colonels and Regiments: Being a History of Iowa Regiments in the War of the Rebellion; and Containing a Description of the Battles in Which They Have Fought* (Des Moines: Mills & Co., 1865).

34 A Member of Co. D, 10th Mo., Glenwood, Mo., "Jackson, Miss.: Who Planted the Flag on the Court-House?" *National Tribune,* 22 January 1885, 3.

Chicago Times correspondent Franc Wilkie described the charge of Crocker's division: "It was a most magnificent charge across that open field; in the face of deadly fire our men never wavered, keeping perfect alignment. Crocker rode on the right of the line, keeping even with it during the charge and going over the works with his men."

Harper's Pictorial History of the Civil War

perfect order," McPherson crowed, the troops cheering wildly as they went.[35]

"Never did lead rain upon charging columns as upon these," said Kenderdine, "and the ground we passed over was covered with our dead and wounded...." Yet, claimed Crocker, "Not a man wavered or faltered, but proceeded, under the most galling fire, to drive the enemy at the point of the bayonet from his strong position."[36] John Sanborn described the charge as "one of the most splendid battle scenes that could ever be witnessed":

---

35 McPherson, 638; Deimling, 782.

36 Crocker, 723.

The whole line, with banners unfurled, went forward at double-quick and with more regularity than at an ordinary battalion drill. The fleeing lines of the rebels in front; the sharpshooters, who had been concealed behind cotton bales and in an old cotton-gin in front of the Fifty-ninth Indiana, throwing out white handkerchiefs at every window and over every cotton bale. . . .[37]

Two batteries—Lt. Julius MacMurray's of the 1st Missouri Light and Capt. Henry Dillon's of the 6th Wisconsin—charged forward close on the infantry's heels, adding to "the novel spectacle" by wheeling into position and firing into the fleeing Confederates. "I am here—open fire on them," Dillion shouted to his men—and they did, all six pieces booming almost simultaneously.[38] Members of Dillon's gun crews even engaged the enemy with their sabers, so close were they. "Seeing this," said Kenderdine, "the infantry cheered and rushed to their support."[39]

"All seemed to seek positions of peril instead of safety," Sanborn added, "and where the enemy was strongest and most secure from danger, there did they charge the fiercest and with the greatest determination."[40] As hyperbolic as Sanborn sounded, it carried at least a note of truth. One Union soldier noticed, "Generals McPherson and Crocker were in the thickest of the fight, taking things as coolly as if there was no danger."[41]

---

37 Sanborn, 729.

38 Jenkin Lloyd Jones, *An Artilleryman's Diary* (Wisconsin History Commission, 1914), 57.

39 Kenderdine, 4.

40 Sanborn, 729.

41 Diary, H.S. Keene, 6th Wisconsin Battery, files VNMP, quoted in Bearss, 544.

The 10th Missouri endured "a terrific fire of shell, canister, and musketry" as it charged. Color Sgt. Calvin Lingle, "although weakened by disease, displayed undaunted courage and determination to keep the flag to the front," Deimling later noted. The Missourians reached the Wright house, "in and behind which, and the hedges, fences, and trees surrounding it, the rebels were hidden and protected." The 24th South Carolina infantry punished the Missourians "severely from the streams of fire which issued from behind every object which could furnish a protection. . . ." As the Missourians got in among them, though, Deimling said "an almost hand-to-hand" fight ensued.[42]

In the melee, Lt. Col. Ellison Capers, commanding the Palmetto State boys, had his horse shot out from under him. He remounted but then was shot through the left leg. Capers didn't realize the severity off the wound until an aide commented on how pale the lieutenant colonel looked. The comment finally drew Capers's attention to his wound, and he noticed for the first time the blood sloshing around in his boot. The loss of blood finally made him faint, but members of his staff evacuated him from the field.[43] He would eventually be promoted to colonel for his efforts at Jackson.

The South Carolinians finally broke on "a dead 'skedaddle'" back toward town.[44] Deimling reformed the regiment for pursuit, but Dillion's battery opened and "completed the rout of the enemy."[45] Artillerist Jenkin Lloyd Jones said, "[W]e were enveloped in a cloud of powder smoke, then another, until nearly all the shells were gone,

---

42 Deimling, O.R. XXIV, Pt. 1, 782-3, 785.

43 Capers, 61, 64.

44 A Member of Co. D, 10th Mo., Glenwood, Mo., "Jackson, Miss.: Who Planted the Flag on the Court-House?" *National Tribune*, 22 January 1885, 3.

45 Deimling, 782-3.

LT. COL. ELLISON CAPERS

Ellison Capers's nickname, "the soldier bishop," came after the war. An 1857 graduate of what is now the Citadel, Ellison served through the war until his capture at Bentonville. After the war, in 1865, he became South Carolina's secretary of state; in 1866, he was ordained as an episcopal priest. In 1894, he was elevated to bishop.

The Soldier-Bishop

when we ceased fire and they were gone."[46] Left behind: "Dead rebels," said Jones, "and many of them lay there wounded and bleeding."[47]

To the left of the Missourians, the 80th Ohio, advancing up the slope as the center of Holmes's three regiments, likewise took "a galling fire" from the Confederates around the Wright house. A picket fence surrounded the home but served as little obstruction to the Buckeyes. "When the 80th reached the fence I never saw pickets fly faster," one witness said; "the fence was demolished and the [Confederate] troops forced to fly."[48]

The 17th Iowa, on the left flank of the formation, took heavy casualties as it charged down the ravine. "[M]y left wing, being unsupported, was exposed to a severe

---

46 Jones, 57.

47 Ibid.

48 Kenderdine, 4. Kenderdine misidentified the Confederates as Floridians, but no Floridians fought in the battle; rather, they were most likely the 24th South Carolina, which had taken up position around the Wright house on the south side of the road.

COL. DAVID BURKE HILLIS
The fight at Jackson would be the "first hard-fought battle" for Col. David Hillis of the 17th Iowa, said one historian; "and his gallant conduct secured the love and admiration of his regiment."

Iowa: Its History and Its Foremost Citizens

cross-fire from the right of the enemy's lines," Hillis later explained. Nonetheless, his bayonet charge at the double-quick drove the Confederates from their line over the crest of the next hill. There, the Iowans found themselves confronted by Confederate artillery not yet evacuated from the field. One gunner discharged a double load of grape and canister at them from a range of about twenty yards, dropping as many as twenty men before the Hawkeyes swarmed in and around the guns.[49] As Confederates fled "at a breakneck gait," the Iowans turned the remaining cannon on them.[50] "I shall always remember the terribly destructive and last shot given by the rebel battery," said a witness from the 80th Ohio.[51]

In the melee, Capt. Littleton W. Huston of the 17th Iowa had his sword-arm shattered but still managed to knock the rifle from the hand of a Confederate sergeant

---

49 Joseph J. Huston, "Who Planted the Flag at Jackson Miss?," *National Tribune,* 19 February 1885, 3.

50 L. F. Parrish, "At Jackson: How the Rebels Were Driven from the Capital of Mississippi," *The National Tribune,* 11 August 1887, 3.

51 Huston, 3.

preparing to fire at him. The gun discharged as it fell. "What are you doing?" Houston demanded.

"Fighting," the Confederate replied.

"Why, you are whipped."

"We have never been whipped before," he answered.[52]

Like the Missourians and Ohioans, the Iowans halted under orders to reform, "panting on the spot but just now wrested from the enemy," a regimental historian said.[53] As they rallied around their colors, they broke into song. "[W]ith all the patriotism, vim and power of voice that they could command, [they] sang that grand old song, 'Yes, We'll Rally Round the Flag, Boys,'" a member of Company G recalled. "I never heard it sung before nor since when it sounded so well nor so appropriate. I expect some of the Johnnies heard the singing, too."

Crocker, himself feeling exuberant, rode up, hat in hand. "God bless you, colonel," he said to Hillis. Looking at the regiment, he added, "Don't let any one tell me the 17th won't fight."[54]

When Crocker's division went forward, Logan's division along the railroad also flexed its muscles, although it turned out to be mostly for show. As Logan himself later attested, "My command was not engaged that day."[55] His mere presence threw off Farquharson, who found himself trapped on the far side of a rain-swollen Town Creek and unable to easily come to Colquitt's support. He might not have anyway, suggests historian Timothy B. Smith, "because he was only under orders to threaten and not attack. . . ."[56] Farquharson evacuated his men from the

---

52 Kenderdine, 4. Kenderdine misidentifies his captain as "Houston."

53 Addision, 327.

54 Stuart, 327.

55 Logan, O.R. XXIV, Pt. 1, 646.

56 Timothy B. Smith, *Champion Hill: Decisive Battle for Vicksburg* (El Dorado Hills, CA: Savas Beatie, 2004), 101.

field and joined Johnston's evacuating column headed northeast. Brig. Gen. John Stevenson, brought up from reserve, arrived "only in time to witness the brilliant and successful charge of the Seventh Division, driving the enemy in dismay from the field"—not realizing it hadn't been much of a charge or much of a drive.[57]

---

57 Stevenson, 717.

8

ALL FIRE AND SPIRIT

AS EVENTS unfolded on McPherson's front northwest of the city, events unfolded simultaneously on Sherman's front to the city's southwest.

Sherman, 43, had not only the benefit of a West Point education, graduating in the Class of 1840, but he came from a politically prominent family. One of the few professional soldiers to recognize early on that the war would be long and ugly, he was harangued for his view and suffered a nervous breakdown. Grant rescued him from the subsequent military purgatory, and thereafter, they worked together and depended on one another closely. If McPherson was Grant's wunderkind, Sherman was his right hand, hammer, alter ego, and go-to guy all in one. "He stood by me when I was crazy, and I stood by him when he was drunk," Sherman would famously say one day; "and now, sir, we stand by each other always."[1]

The two stood by each other on the downpour morning of May 14, too, with Grant and Sherman making headquarters together on the advance from Mississippi Springs, a few miles east of Raymond. Brig. Gen. James Tuttle led the way, his steadily advancing skirmish line easily plowing

---

1 Linus Pierpont Brockett, *Our Great Captains: Grant, Sherman, Thomas, Sheridan, and Farragut* (New York: Charles B. Richardson, 1865), 162.

COL. ALBERT THOMPSON
A pre-war lawyer in Paducah, Kentucky, Albert Thompson would be killed just two blocks from his home during a March 1864 raid on Paducah led by Nathan Bedford Forrest.

Jason Voigt/Historical Marker Database

forward against Gregg's light resistance, routing them from cover.[2] "It was a novel sight to see our skirmishers contending every inch of the ground before an overwhelming force to see them load and fire, and gradually falling back, facing the advancing foe," said one Confederate observer.[3]

About two and a half miles out of Jackson, though, where the road crossed Lynch Creek, the opposition suddenly stiffened—"a heavier force with artillery, which immediately opened on us," Tuttle said.[4]

Col. Albert P. Thompson of the 3rd Kentucky Mounted Infantry—part of Gregg's force from Port Hudson—commanded the Confederate forces south of the city. He had placed his Kentuckians on the west side of the road and the Georgians on the east, with the four guns of Martin's Georgia Battery in the middle on the road itself. Thompson had fewer than 1,000 men to contest the advance of Sherman's 10,000. As woefully outnumbered

---

2   Miles, "Capture of Jackson," 3 August 1893.

3   Isaac Hermann, *Memoirs of a Veteran who Served as a Private in the 60's in the War Between the States: Personal Incidents, Experiences, and Observations* (Atlanta: Byrd Printing Company, 1911), 103.

4   Tuttle, O.R. XXIV, Pt. 1, 759.

Lynch Creek isn't wide, but its banks are steep, which means it gets deep quickly when rain waters swell the stream, making it functionally impossible to ford.

Chris Mackowski

---

as he was, Thompson knew he could bottleneck the Federal column at the bridge.

Lynch Creek, "winding in muddy swirls and many meanderings across the level meadows," according to one observer, had swollen to an unfordable depth from the night's torrential rain.[5] Coupled with "its precipitous banks," as Sherman called them, the creek "could only be passed on the bridge. . . ."[6] Inspecting the situation for

---

5 Robert J. Burdette, *The Drums of the 47th* (Indianapolis, IN: The Bobbs-Merrill Company, 1914), 49. Burdette became a well-known American humorist after the war and, later, a minister. His second wife, Clara, published *Drums* in 1914 following his death.

6 Sherman, 753.

BRIG. GENS. JOSEPH MOWER AND CHARLES MATTHIES

Joseph Mower may have commanded the "Live Eagle Brigade," but he earned a nickname of his own, "The Wolf," for actions at the battle of Iuka in September 1862. He earned another, "The Swamp Lizard," for his crossing of the Salkehatchie River near Columbia, South Carolina, in February 1865. *Library of Congress*

Prussian-born Charles Leopold Matthies had experience in the Prussian army before emigrating to Iowa. His grave in Burlington proclaims him to be the first person in the state—and perhaps the country to tender his services to the United States for the war. *Library of Congress*

himself, Sherman directed Brig. James Tuttle to deploy Brig. Gen. Joseph Mower's brigade to the right of the road and Matthies's brigade to the left, with Brig. Gen. Ralph Buckland's brigade between and behind them as a reserve.

Robert J. Burdette, a private in the 47th Illinois—part of Mower's Brigade—was a new recruit going into his first battle. "I called it a battle," he clarified. "The

PVT. ROBERT BURDETTE
Robert Burdette served as a private in the 47th Illinois during the Civil War. Later in life, he became a nationally renowned humorist, best known for "The Rise and Fall of the Mustache."

Library of Congress

old soldiers spoke of it as a fight."[7] Burdette described "A dull staccato thunder of guns in the distant front [from McPherson's corps]," and then

a galloping staff-orderly giving an order to Colonel [John] Cromwell, which he shouted to us; a sudden barking of many commands from the line officers; a double-quicking of the column into the line, and almost in the time I have written it we were in line of battle in the woods before Jackson, Mississippi.

Skirmishers disappeared into the scrub oaks as their captain, Frank Biser, ordered them onward with continuous, "emphatically sulphurous" yelling.

"[S]uddenly they emerged from the woods, where they were concealed," said Confederate artillerist Isaac Hermann, "and advanced in platoon form, sending their deadly missiles into our thin skirmishers ranks." Hermann, caught by surprise even though he professed to

---

7   This and the rest of Burdette's account from *Drums of the 47th*, 49-50.

have been following the action closely, said, "This is more than our men can stand."[8]

As Tuttle's infantry deployed, he also brought two batteries to the front, Battery E of the 1st Illinois Light Artillery and the 2nd Iowa Battery—12 guns in all.[9] Burdette reported hearing the 2nd Iowa far to the right, "its bronze Napoleons throbbing like a heart of fire," and on the left, the Waterhouse Battery of Chicago, "baying like a wolf-hound at the gray battalions. . . ." The 47th moved in support of the Chicagoans.

It was "a grand, sublime scene," said one Wisconsinite, also in the brigade.[10] According to another, caught up in the moment:

> [T]he heavy booming of cannon away to the left, where McPherson is engaging the enemy, with the shells bursting around us, the rapid fire of musktey [sic] and a storm of leaden hail sweeping by, blending with the almost incessant lightning and thunder crash of heaven's artillery, with the down-pouring torrents from the clouds—all combine to make a scene of sublime but rather dismal grandeur.[11]

Hermann, too, from his position with Martin's Georgia Battery, made note of the weather, although in a different way: the Federal fire "rattled through the tree tops like hail."

> One of their shots passed over my gun and knocked it off its sight, passed between the detachment, striking the caisson

---

8   Hermann, 103-4.

9   Bearss, 535.

10   George W. Driggs, *Opening of the Mississippi; or, Two Years' Campaigning in the South-West. A Record of the Campaigns, Sieges, Actions and March in which the 8th Wisconsin Volunteers have Participated* (Madison, IS: Wm J. Park & Co., 1864), 133.

11   Miles, "Capture of Jackson," *The National Tribune,* 3 August 1893.

lid in the rear and staving it in, and thus preventing us for a few minutes in replying. We had to break it open with hand spikes to get ammunition. . . . [W]e resumed business again, and they came back at us. I saw a ball rolling on the ground, about six feet to my right. It seemed to be about the same caliber as ours. It rolled up a stump, bouncing about fifteen feet in the air. I thought it was a solid shot and[,] wanting to send it back to them through the muzzle of our gun, I ran after it. It proved to be a shell, as it exploded, and a piece of it struck my arm. It was a painful wound, but not serious. Another ball struck a tree about eight inches in diameter, knocked out a chip, which struck my face and caused me to see the seven stars in plain day light. . . .[12]

The conversation between artillerists, one-sided, lasted 20 minutes. Thompson's men, says historian Edwin Bearss, "had the unhappy choice of remaining in the open and being pounded to bits by the superior Union artillery, or retreating to fight again under more favorable conditions."[13] Thompson made the understandable decision to withdraw, but he did so without destroying the bridge behind him. Drenched as it was, perhaps the wood would not burn in the storm. "The Rebels thus abandoned the only position they could hope to hold," says Bearss: "an unfordable stream to their front with a wooden bridge across it."[14]

Isaac Hermann had been tasked with passing the withdrawal order down the Confederate line. Using the color bearer's horse—"a fine animal" named "Stonewall"—he spread the word. During his mission, he encountered a member of his gun crew, Slim Bland. "Slim, this is a hot time," Hermann shouted. Before Bland could reply, a solid

[12] Hermann, 105, 104-5.

[13] Ibid, 537-9.

[14] Ibid., 537.

ISAAC HERMANN
Isaac Hermann, who rose to the rank of captain, would serve in all three branches of the army by the time the war ended.

Memoirs of a Veteran

shot struck him, tearing his left side "entirely to pieces." Hermann paused to try and save the body, but with Confederate counterbattery fire withdrawing, Federal gunners were having free reign. Hermann collected what he could of Bland's personal items, which he later returned to Bland's brother.[15]

The bridge over Lynch Creek did bottleneck Sherman as expected, but Sherman found the single choke point a better option than trying to cross the rain-swollen creek. His men poured over the span and then, like sand dropping through the neck of an hourglass, began to fan out on the north side of the creek, this time with Mower's and Matthies's positions reversed. As the Federals deployed, "Task Force Thompson" fell back to a skirt of woods just outside the scant earthworks that ringed the town.[16] Behind the works, Mississippi State Troops and civilian volunteers bolstered their ranks. Ten additional pieces of artillery added weight to those of the Georgians, giving Confederates a 14-to-12 advantage in cannon.

---

15 Hermann, 105.

16 Bearss coins the term "Taskforce Thompson," 536.

The two sides then proceeded to psych each other out. Burdette admired the "long line of gray-jacketed skirmishers doing a beautiful skirmish drill. Puff-puff-puff the little clouds of blue smoke broke out from the gray line. . . ." Then, in turn, he saw "the blue-bloused skirmish line come into view from the woods at the foot of the hill." A back-and-forth unfolded between the opposing sides:

> I saw the skirmishers now and then rush suddenly together, rallying by fours and squads as a little troop of cavalry [mounted infantry] menaced the line with a rush—a charge, we called it then. I saw them deploy just as quickly, and heard them cheering as a rapid volley admonished the troopers with a few empty saddles. Then I saw the gray line advance resolutely, with much dodging and zigzagging our own skirmishers were slowly falling back to their line of support.[17]

Burdette watched the scene from his regiment's position near the 1st Illinois Light Artillery. Nearby, a young artilleryman, not more than nineteen years old, was half-seated on the hub of one of his guns, then cooling down. His face rested on his arm, which served as a cushion on the rim of the wheel. "He was tired," Burdette noted, "for serving the guns in hot action is fast work and hard work." Another of the gunners made a comment—Burdette didn't hear what—and the young artilleryman lifted his face and smiled, his face "handsome in its animation," Burdette said. "[A] beautiful boy." And just then

> I heard a sound such as I had never heard before, but I shuddered as I heard it,—dull and cruel and deadly. A hideous sound, fearsome and hateful.

17 Burdette, 50-2.

The young artilleryman leaped to his feet, his face toward the gray sky, his hands tossed above his head. He reeled, and as a comrade sprang to catch him in his arms the boy cried, his voice shrilling down the line:

"Murder, boys! Murder! Oh, murder!"

He clasped his hands over a splotch of crimson that was widening on the blue breast of his red-trimmed jacket and fell into the strong arms of the comrades who carried him to the rear. Him, or—It. . . .

Alive, the artilleryman had been a "Him"; as a corpse, was he suddenly an "It," Burdette wondered. Everything, it seemed, had changed. "Fear, before unfelt because unknown, clutched my heart like the hand of death, with the voice of that hissing spiteful bullet," he admitted. "My very soul was faint."[18]

As more of Sherman's infantry crossed the bridge, the size of the blue host intimidated Thompson's men into slipping into the works rather than making a stand just outside them—a smart decision under any circumstance. The rain made even that simple maneuver a challenge, though. "The horses stalled," said Hermann. "The road being very muddy, the men had to assist at the wheel to pull the carriages out of the mud, by using all their efforts. . . ."[19]

Meanwhile, the sight of the works gave Federals reason to pause in their advance. "As we emerged from the woods," Sherman recalled, "to our front and as far to the left as we could see, appeared a line of entrenchments, and the enemy kept up a pretty brisk fire with artillery from the points that enfiladed our road."[20]

---

18 Ibid., 52-3.

19 Hermann, 107.

20 Sherman, 753.

CAPT. JULIUS PITZMAN
Prussian-born Julius Pitzman had a background in civil and topographical engineering rather than military engineering but nonetheless volunteered his services at the start of the war.

Author's collection

Rather than charge headlong into who-knew-what, Sherman decided to find out "what." Grant, who came up to inspect the situation for himself, agreed. They retired to the porch of a small cottage immediately behind Matthies's brigade, and Sherman called for Capt. Julius Pitzman, acting chief engineer for the corps. Pitzman's mission: take the 95th Ohio on a recon to the right and see if he could find the Confederate flank or any weakness in the line.

As they conferred, Confederate artillerists honed in on the cluster of horses in front of the cottage, which suggested a cluster of officers. "Several Confederate shells endangered their lives," Matthies noted.[21] The hazard soon passed: Pitzman left on his mission and Grant and Sherman mounted their horses and rode among the men, offering encouragement.[22]

The 95th Ohio, accompanying Pitzman, came from Buckland's brigade, coming up from reserve to bolster Tuttle. Buckland's men advanced in line across an open field, crossed a ravine "which proved to be deeper than was supposed," Buckland said, and then came out into

---

21 Matthies, 770.

22 Frederick Dent Grant, "A Boy's Experience at Vicksburg," *Personal Recollections of the War of the Rebellion*, Military Order of the Loyal Legion of the United States—New York, 3rd Series, 92.

BRIG. GEN.
RALPH BUCKLAND
Prior to the war, Ralph Buckland was law partners with future U. S. President Rutherford B. Hayes.

Library of Congress

an open field directly in front of a Confederate artillery emplacement.[23] With no cover, Buckland withdrew his men into the woods where they endured a barrage for nearly an hour. "[T]he enemy's batteries . . . were served with admirable precision," Buckland grimaced. It was the first time two of his regiments, the 93rd Indiana and 114th Illinois, had ever been under fire. Col. DeWitt C. Thomas, leading the Indianans, said his regiment suffered considerably from the shells. "[A]lthough they were exploding incessantly for over an hour, my men and officers stood like old veterans, the shell doing execution at every explosion," he reported.[24] Buckland lauded the "officers and men [who] behaved with the coolness of veterans. Not a man left his post."

On the right, Pitzman's expedition intersected with the tracks of the New Orleans, Jackson, and Great Northern Railroad, running north-south, providing a direct line into the city. As the 95th Ohio advanced up the

---

23 This and other Buckland quotes in this paragraph come from Buckland, O.R. XXIV, Pt. 1, 762.

24 DeWitt, O.R. XXIV, Pt. 1, 764.

rail line, they soon came up on a rebel camp—deserted—and then a long line of rifle pits—also deserted. It took the Buckeyes a moment to realize it, but they had just broken through the Confederate works. "Here I formed my line and planted my colors in full view of the city," said Col. William L. McMillen.[25]

The commotion attracted the attention of one of the black residents of the city. The Confederates had evacuated, he told them, with the exception of a small number of soldiers left to work a battery that was firing on the main Federal position. "I moved my regiment rapidly through a street in the suburbs and gained its rear," McMillen said.

John F. Bowen, a member of the regiment, recalled then reaching the rear of a large farm house, "on one side of which was a rebel battery firing at our men in the woods in front of them as fast as they could. Between them and us was a very thick hedge fence which concealed us from them, although we were within some 50 yards of the battery when we were ordered to charge, which we did. . . ."[26] In their swift descent, they scooped up nine guns and 52 prisoners.

Pitzman, meanwhile, returned to headquarters to report what his expedition had found. Sherman responded by sending Maj. Gen. Frederick Steele's entire division, just then coming up behind Tuttle's, over to the railroad to follow-up the 95th's breakthrough.

Even as the 95th Ohio found its way past the Confederate flank, Mower, looking closely at the works opposite the main Federal position, realized how thinly defended they were. "We can take those works and not half try," he said.[27] The sound of fighting from the rear

---

25 This and the account that follows comes from McMillen, O.R. XXIV, Pt. 1, 766.

26 J. F. Bowen, "The First Flag at Jackson, Miss.," *The National Tribune*, 1 January 1885, 8.

27 Woodworth, 102.

of the position—the 95th's attack-from-behind on the artillery battery—seemed to confirm the assessment. "[A]s soon as I heard the cheers of his men," Sherman recalled, "Tuttle was ordered in by the main road."[28]

Pvt. S. C. Miles of the 8th Wisconsin, part of Mower's brigade, recalled "the battle's din of booming cannons' roar and bursting shell" and then, ringing along the line, the command, "Attention! Fix bayonets—Forward—Double-quick—Now, steady, boys! Keep your alignment—March!"[29] Mower himself led the charge and, according to Tuttle, "displayed great coolness and bravery."[30]

Not everyone followed the commander's example. Capt. John T. Bowen of the 47th Illinois's Company A, along with an unidentified second lieutenant, both deserted. Sergeant John Watts "rallied the men as they hesitated under a terrific fire, and by waving his hat and cheering succeeded in moving them forward in gallant style, himself leading," recounted Tuttle in recommending Watts's promotion to take Bowen's place.[31] Sherman, endorsing the recommendation, said such events "develop the true soldierly qualities."[32]

The rest of the 47th, though, answered "the sweet and imperious bugle call," said one member of the regiment, "and with mighty shouting rushed forward like unleashed dogs of war." Amidst thundering guns, rattling musketry, "cheering and more cheering," it was, he said, "a triumphant charge, a wild pursuit, a mad dash. . . ."[33]

---

28 Sherman, 754.

29 Miles, "Capture of Jackson," *The National Tribune,* 3 August 1893, 3.

30 Tuttle, O.R. XXIV, Pt. 1, 760.

31 Ibid.

32 Sherman endorsement of Tuttle report, Tuttle, O.R. XXIV, Pt. 1, 761.

33 Burdette, 57.

PVT. SAMUEL C. MILES
"[A]s springs, rivulets, brooks and creeks combine to form great rivers, so the incidents of personal endurance, daring and heroism of the private soldier are indispensable to the accomplishment of the great events," wrote Pvt. S. C. Miles in his postwar memoir of the Live Eagle Brigade. Miles, of Springdale, Iowa, described himself in the book as both "a high private in the ranks" and as "the hospital patient," and had himself sketched as such.

An Epic on "Old Abe,"
The War Eagle

THE HOSPITAL PATIENT.

"[W]ith bayonets fixed and with exultant shouts the line moved forward at a run," said Col. Lucius F. Hubbard of the 5th Minnesota. It was, added Wisconsinite George Driggs, "a rush and a yell that would have frightened the savages. . . ."[34] Driggs painted a scene of the army in motion: "our banners are unfurled to the breeze, and notwithstanding we have made a fatiguing march of some nine miles, over heavy roads, the men are eager for the affray [sic]."[35]

"Swift as a mountain avalanche, swifter, swiftest, was that 'Forward,'" said John Melvin Williams, also of the 8th Wisconsin.[36]

---

34 Driggs, 133.

35 Ibid.

36 John Melvin Williams, *The "Eagle Regiment,": 8th Wis. Inf'ty. Vols.* (Belleville, WI: Recorder Print, 1890), 58.

Miles, in swollen-purple prose, recounted an onward sweep of an "irresistible line of blue"...

> undismayed and unchecked by the terrible storm of lead and iron which thins their ranks and strews the field with mangled slain. With their thundering Union cheer pealing clear above the battle's horrid din, as their undaunted line sweeps up that last homestretch of bristling trench and parapet-crowned hights [sic], is it any wonder that when they leap over those defenses they find most of that chivalrous line in full flight for safer localities. . . ?[37]

"It was soon discovered . . . that the enemy had evacuated," wrote Hubbard more soberly. The charge, he said in contrast to Miles, was "a bloodless one."[38] Aside from a few civilian defenders, not a Confederate soldier could be found.

The difference between Hubbard's account and Miles's is best explained by the presence of the brigade's mascot, "Old Abe" the War Eagle. As his official report, written at the time of the battle, Hubbard offered a straightforward recap. Miles, on the other hand, was one of several veterans of the 8th Wisconsin who wrote postwar biographies of the famous mascot—who came from their regiment—and in the interest of selling books in a crowded market, they made their stories as exciting as possible—although, like the hyperbolic Miles, each claimed "to present a true narrative of incidents."[39]

---

37 Miles, "Capture of Jackson," 3 August 1893.

38 Hubbard, 768.

39 S. C. Miles, *An Epic on "Old Abe," The War Eagle* (Stetsonville, WI: The War Eagle Book Association, 1894), 5. A fragment of the manuscript exists in the Wisconsin Historical Society online collection. (https://content.wisconsinhistory.org/digital/collection/quiner/id/41362). For more on the colorful Miles, see Chris Mackowski, "The Battle of Jackson—and Off to Moscow!" *The Summer of '63: Vicksburg and Tullahoma* (Savas Beatie, 2021).

Old Abe the War Eagle, tethered to his perch, went into battle along with the brigade's colors.

An Epic on "Old Abe," The War Eagle

George W. Driggs wrote the first regimental history of the 8th in 1864, but it covered only the first two years of the regiment's service. In 1890, John Melvin Williams took up the task of writing a more complete account, "so well begun" by Driggs.[40] While Abe appeared in Driggs's book, Williams really played up Abe as "the embodiment of a sublime fury."[41] At the battle of Jackson, Williams wrote, "A violent storm poured out its vials of wrath upon friend and foe. Gazing at the heavens, the eyes of the Eagle seemed as lightning. . . ." Like a holy aspergillum, "when [Abe] stretched [his pinions] forth and dashed the electric

---

40 Williams, ix.

41 Ibid, 58.

drops of rain upon the soldiers, they were inspired with an inexpressible enthusiasm."[42]

By then, Williams was competing against several other bios of Abe written by fellow members of the regiment, including Joseph O. Barrett's *History of "Old Abe,": the Live War Eagle of the Eighth Regiment Wisconsin Volunteers* (1865) and Frank Abial Flower's *Old Abe, the Eighth Wisconsin War Eagle* (1885).

"The scene at the battle of Jackson, Miss., was such as to afford a revelry of delight to the wild and stormy spirit of an eagle," wrote Flower.

> The federal attack was impetuous, but nature's battle—the attack of the elements—was even fiercer. The swift movements of the troops, dashing rain, the rush and roar of battle, the flash of lightning and the peal of thunder, all overhung by a black and angry sky that reached heavily down to mingle with the smoke of the conflict, combined to make a scene of sublimity which man is not often permitted to witness.[43]

During the storm, "Abe was all spirit and fire," Flower said. "He flapped his pinions and sent his powerful scream high above the din of battle."

Miles probably takes top honors for his purple-prosed descriptions, though. His late-to-the-party accounts in the *National Tribune* didn't come until 1893, and his book, *An Epic on "Old Abe," The War Eagle,* came in 1894. Coming on the tailwinds of the others, his needed to be the most spectacular account of all in order to compete. "And now," he wrote of Mowers's assault at Jackson,

---

42 Ibid.

43 Flower, 38.

out upon the open field sweeps that invincible line of loyal blue and vengeful glistening steel . . . [toward] the unquailing, even line of valiant defenders. . . . [B]eneath one of those four stands of proudly-waving regimental banners the War Eagle Old Abe's valiant form and spreading wings proclaim to that line of rebel gray that they are vainly resisting a foe who never knew defeat.[44]

Embellishments for literary effect aside, these Abe the Eagle admirers all captured some basic truths about the role of the brigade and the battle of Jackson. "The federals won," wrote Flower, "and Old Abe, with the 'lightning playing on his pinions,' entered the capital of Mississippi at the head of the victorious army."[45]

---

44 Miles, "Capture of Jackson," 3 August 1893, 3.

45 Flower, 38.

9

Good-Night at the Stars

AT THE northwest corner of the city, McPherson's men were making the same discovery Sherman's men were making on the southwest corner. Skirmishers from all three of Holmes's regiments eased forward. At first, Confederate artillerists from earthworks on a ridge on the outskirts of town opened "a brisk fire," but things soon fell silent.[1] The enemy "had fled in great confusion abandoning his position and camp, fort, containing four pieces of artillery," reported Col. Hillis of the 17th Iowa.[2] After the grief doled out on the Iowans by Confederate artillery less than an hour earlier, the four unspiked guns made poetic spoils.

"Cheer after cheer went up from the infantry as McPherson went galloping by," one Federal artillerist recalled. "I never before could see how men should cheer on the battlefield, but I never felt more like it in my life. Such is victory."[3]

McPherson and Sherman had coordinated their plan so well that they'd opened the fight on their respective fronts almost simultaneously. Their troop dispositions took almost the same amount of time, as did their

1 Deimling, 783.

2 Hillis, 778.

3 Jones, 57.

COL. PEYTON COLQUITT
Peyton Colquitt demonstrated a never-say-quit attitude at Jackson. At the same time, his older brother, Alfred, was serving as a brigadier under Stonewall Jackson in the Army of Northern Virginia, although Alfred's performance at Chancellorsville raised doubts about his effectiveness.

Library of Congress

initial assaults against Confederate defenders. The pauses in each fight also came at about the same time—and during those pauses, at around 2:00 p.m.—Gregg received word that the evacuation of supplies was complete.

"I immediately ordered the entire force to withdraw," he reported, "which was done in excellent order, our troops not having permitted the enemy to press them back at any point until the order was given."[4] Colquitt likewise exaggerated his success, "not a man having receded an inch, and having resisted successfully the column of the enemy."[5] Walker, "furious at [having] been obliged to evacuate Jackson after having only destroyed four hundred Yankees," later told observer Arthur Fremantle, "I know I couldn't hold the place, but I did want to kill a few more of the rascals."[6]

---

4 Gregg, 786.

5 Colquitt, O.R. XXIV, Pt. 1, 787.

6 Fremantle, 117.

Despite their inflationary accounts, all three Confederate officers *had* helped lead highly successful delaying actions, buying Johnston the necessary time to lead the army's supply train in northward retreat. In their withdrawals, the two wings of Gregg's force "came into their proper places from the different roads without interference" from each other and smoothly settled into the retreat column streaming from the city. Thompson's mounted infantry and Capt. T. M. Nelson's company of cavalry brought up the rear.[7]

Johnston didn't seem to appreciate the value of Gregg's stand, though. "The necessity of taking the Canton road at right angles to that upon which the enemy approached prevented an obstinate defense," he wrote to Pemberton, underselling the importance of Gregg's action in allowing his clean getaway.[8]

Meanwhile, to hear the Wisconsinites in Mower's brigade tell it, they flushed the remnants of Confederate resistance from the city all on their own. "Having cleared and captured the defenses of Jackson on the southwest, the Live Eagle Brigade pursues the retreating Confederates through the streets to the north . . ." wrote Miles, who called it a "hurried vacation by the enemy" that "compelled the hasty evacuation of those in front of McPherson's Corps on the Clinton road . . ."[9] Driggs recalled a regimental sprint "through the streets of the city on double quick, amid the wild huzzas of the victors."[10]

As the Confederates left Jackson—of their own volition, claims of the Live Eagles notwithstanding—they torched the remaining warehouses, still brimming with a

---

7   Gregg, 786.

8   Johnston to Pemberton, 877.

9   Miles, "Capture of Jackson," 3 August 1893, 3.

10 Driggs, 133.

large amount of commissary stores.[11] A few miles outside of town, "W" of the routed 14th Mississippi paused to look back: "[O]ver the doomed city, a tall column of black smoke was slowly unfolding into a huge umbrella; and a sound, like the distant murmur of the sea, broke on my ear." He had said that "Jackson was abandoned to the torch of the invader," but in fact, some of the first "invaders" into town set to work extinguishing the fires.

Artillerist Isaac Hermann, suffering from a wounded foot as well as the jolt he'd received in the battle from the exploding shell, was among the stragglers scrambling out of the city as the Federals flooded in. "On my way down the street a lady was standing over a tub of whiskey with a dipper in her hand. . . . She dipped up a dipper full of whiskey, which I drank . . ." he admitted. "It was the medicine I surely needed."[12]

Men from Logan's division came up along the railroad and tried to pursue the retreating Confederate column, but the Confederates' head start coupled with the muddy roads left Logan's exhausted men unable to catch them. A strong push might have bagged at least some of them, though. "I never saw so many broken-down men as on that evening," wrote Pvt. W. J. Davidson of the 41st Tennessee. "The mud and our wet clothing and blankets, together with a day's fasting and a very hard march on the previous night, were too much for us." The fight, he admitted, "was a very poor affair after all. . . ."[13]

11 Grant, *Memoirs*, 337-8.

12 Hermann, 109. In the interest of full disclosure: Published in 1911, Hermann's memoir often reads like a boy's adventure tale. The book is definitely entertaining, but at times, it reads as though Hermann alternatively saved Confederate forces single-handedly or wasn't fighting at all because he was busy having Tom Sawyer-esque adventures behind the lines. I've tried to use excerpts that realistically and logically place him in the action where he wasn't placing himself *as* the action.

13 Davidson, 170.

The column "trudged along in the mud for six miles and then struck camp," wrote Flavel C. Barber of the 3rd Tennessee. Despite the soaking-wet ground, Barber and his retreating comrades were "in high spirits because Old Joe was with us." Not privy to the politics of command, soldiers felt buoyed by Johnston's reputation. "Of our future operations of course we know nothing," Barber wrote in his journal on May 15. "Our men are very tired but still in good spirits and have the most unbounded confidence in General Johnston."[14]

As the Confederates withdrew, the Federals poured in from the southwest and northwest. As John Sanborn's brigade advanced into town, Capt. Lucien B. Martin, Sanborn's acting assistant adjutant-general, rode up to the leading regiment, the 59th Indiana, and asked for the regimental colors. Col. Jesse Alexander acquiesced and, riding far in advance of the skirmishers, Martin placed the colors on the dome of the capitol, where they remained in charge of the regiment's color-guard. "They were the first and only colors planted on the capitol of Jackson," Alexander crowed, and they remained above the capitol dome until the regiment moved out the following day.[15]

But it was that very timing that made the 59th's claim suspect, argued Wisconsinite S. C. Miles. "Gen. McPherson leaves accordingly early on the morning of the 15th with his corps, and takes Col. Sanborn with him instead of instructing him to plant his regimental flag on the Statehouse dome. . . ." Miles, of course, instead had his own tale of the 8th Wisconsin raising its flag over the capitol. "The line of march of the Live Eagle regiment through the streets of Jackson in pursuit of the fleeing Confederates brings them to the State House Square,

---

14 Flavel C. Barber, *Holding the Line: The Third Tennessee Infantry, 1861-1864*, Robert H. Ferrell, ed. (Kent, OH: Kent State University Press), 122.

15 Alexander, 772. See also Sanborn, 730.

"We tore down the rebel flag from the dome of the state house and placed our own proud banner there, where in triumph it floated during our stay in town," insisted George Driggs, historian of the 8th Wisconsin—one of several regiments to claim the honor of flying their flag above the capitol.

Harper's Weekly

where the Confederate flag is arrogantly waving above the State capitol dome," he said. "It does not take the Color Guard of the Live Eagle regiment many minutes to enter the building and haul down the Secession rag, and about 3 o'clock in the afternoon of May 14, 1863, the Stars and Stripes of the 8th Wis. are proudly waving in its place. . . ."[16] And if that wasn't "America!" enough, the regiment put its bald eagle on proud display out front. Wrote mascot biographer Frank Flower, "Old Abe, the living emblem of our free and undivided country, perched on his shield of stars and stripes, was placed in the beautiful park in front of the steps of the beautiful capitol building, on which, in other days, hundreds of human beings had been sold at auction in hopeless slavery. What a contrast!"[17]

For decades, veterans refought the story of "Who Planted the Flag on the State-House in Jackson" in the pages of outlets such as the *National Tribune*.[18] "Indeed so insistent were the claims," suggests historian Steven Woodworth, "as to raise the question of whether some of

---

16 Miles, "Capture of Jackson," 3 August 1893, 3.

17 Flower, 39.

18 See many of the *National Tribune* articles cited for this piece for examples.

the Federals might have mistaken the Jackson city hall for the state capitol."[19]

Also lost to history was the Confederate flag that flew atop the statehouse before the multitude of supposed replacements, although its place in history was a near miss: Grant's twelve-year-old son nearly captured it. Sylvanus Cadwallader, a journalist for the *Chicago Times* close with Grant, described young Fred as "a stout goodnatured son of the General who accompanied the army all through the campaign." When the army entered the city, Cadwallader and Fred spotted the Confederate flag above the capitol and decided to make a dash for it.

"We supposed ourselves far in advance of anyone connected with the Union army," Cadwallader recalled. Arriving at the capitol, they hitched the horses and bolted upstairs. As they reached the staircase that ascended to the flagpole, they met "a ragged, muddy, begrimed cavalryman descending with the coveted prize under his arm"—perhaps misidentifying the soldier's branch of service. In any case, their disappointment was "extreme." "We were beaten and compelled to admit that to the victor belongs the spoils," Cadwallader said.[20]

Inside the capitol, Fred explored, eventually finding his way to the governor's room, hastily abandoned. "Finding what I supposed to be the governor's pipe lying on the table, I confiscated it," Fred later admitted, "primarily and ostensibly for the national service, but secondarily and actually for my own private individual use." And, he added, "It had the advantage of being still loaded and lighted."[21]

---

19 Woodworth, 105.

20 Sylvanus Cadwallader, *Three Years with Grant*, Benjamin P. Thomas, ed. (Lincoln, NE: Bison Books, 1996), 73-4.

21 Frederick Dent Grant, 93.

Soon after coming out of the building, Fred saw his father approach the statehouse, surrounded by staff. Grant set up headquarters at the Bowman House directly across the street. "I slept that night in the room that Johnston was said to have occupied the night before," Grant later reported.[22]

Cadwallader, too, found a room in the Bowman House where he started cranking out dispatches for the paper, although he had to run a "gauntlet of unfriendly observation" to reach his accommodations. The hotel's office and corridors were

> filled with Confederate officers and soldiers, some of whom were wounded and disabled men from convalescent hospitals; others who were doubtless bummers, skulkers, and deserters who fell out of the Confederate ranks as Johnston's army retreated across the river; and a large concourse of townspeople and civilians who chanced to be there from other parts of the state.[23]

Panicked and outraged citizens soon besieged Grant and, getting little satisfaction from a man with little time or little patience, they shifted their complaints to the provost-marshal, Lt. Col. John W. Jefferson of the 8th Wisconsin, who occupied the state treasurer's office. It was "crowded day and night with citizens and refugees seeking protection from the military officers of the Government they have outraged, defied, and insulted," observed Pvt. Miles, relishing the irony.[24]

Jefferson was not the only officer to take advantage of ersatz government housing, Miles noted:

---

22 Grant, *Memoirs*, 338.

23 Cadwallader, 74.

24 S. C. Miles, "Capture of Jackson," *The National Tribune*, 3 August 1893, 3.

Gen. Mower . . . occupies the Supreme Court room in the capital. Col Robbins, in command of the 8th Wis., temporarily fills the office of the Judges of Errors and Appeals. Col Webber, of the 11th Mo. . . . fills the office of Secretary of State. Col. Hubbard, of the 5th Minn., takes the Attorney-General's Office, and Col. Cromwell, 47th Ill., usurpes [sic] the office of the State Librarian.[25]

Sherman and his staff occupied "a magnificent dwelling near the center of the city" not far from the Bowman House.[26]

Pandemonium held sway in those first hours of the city's fall. "The negroes, poor whites—and it must be admitted—some stragglers and bummers from the ranks of the Union army—carried off thousands of dollars worth of property from houses, homes, shops, and stores . . ." Cadwallader observed. "The streets were filled with people, white and black, who were carrying away all the stolen goods they could stagger under, without the slightest attempt at concealment. . . ." Sherman mainly put a stop to it, but "the era of stealing and plundering lasted through the evening and night of the 14th. . . ."[27]

"If there was a jubilant army, Grant's army at Jackson was that night . . ." said artillerist Jenkin Lloyd Jones. Men foraged for food and supplies. Some tried drying the day's rain from their uniforms. Others rested. "The papers of the morning were found, which said that the Yankee vandals would never pollute Jackson," Jones wrote with obvious appreciation, "having scared [Confederates] out of the capital of one of the strongest states of the Union."[28]

25 Ibid.

26 Ibid.

27 Cadwallader, 75.

28 Jones, 57.

Jones was not the only Federal to savor the Confederate comeuppance. "Each individual man seemed to feel it to be the proudest day of his life as the old flag of our regiment was unfurled to the breeze in the capital city of the rebel President's own State," wrote Hubbard of the 5th Minnesota. "Even the tattered and faded emblem itself seemed to feel inspired by the occasion, and shook its folds more grandly than ever as a response to the scornful glances of the conquered traitors of this rebellious capital."[29]

The 12th Iowa, ordered to "protect themselves against attack," happened to establish bivouac near a large number of cotton bales, which the men soon appropriated and opened up to use them for beds. "For the first time in the service," wrote Lt. David Reed, "many of the men slept on 'downey bed,' their uniforms the next morning bearing evidence that they had 'been in the cotton.'"[30]

Ralph Buckland's brigade also received orders to encamp in a defensive position. Greeted so warmly by artillery on the southwest edge of town, the brigade first bivouacked in a nearby grove next to the Raymond Road but was then ordered to change positions. "[T]he men had got pretty comfortably fixed for drying their clothes, having marched most of the day in a drenching rain," he said, "when I received an order to post my brigade along the rifle-pits, in position to man them in case of attack. This was pretty hard for men who had marched all day in the rain with very little to eat, the rain still continuing at intervals."[31]

The 17th Iowa, which knew a little something about having it "pretty hard" after their charge through the

---

29 Hubbard, O.R. XXIV, Pt. 1, 768.

30 Reed, 119.

31 Buckland, 762.

ravine earlier in the day, now had it a little easier. "That night we camped in Jackson, held a mock Legislature, and passed an act to pay the boys off," said L. E. Parrish, "which was done in Confederate scrip, there being any quantity of it, and if it had been worth anything we would have been rich. But the boys were pretty extravagant, and they would use a $500 or a $1,000 bill to light a pipe or cigar. Tobacco and cigars were plenty here, and all who indulged in the weed laid in a supply."[32]

Federals had some company in the capitol, too. "The legislative halls are occupied by prisoners of war who are present at all hours with a full quorum," noted Miles, "and no filibustering is indulged in to defeat or delay business, but all are alert to devise the best means of bettering their deplorably-degenerate seceded State."[33]

Even men who'd not gotten into the day's fight felt ebullient. "To-night the stars and stripes float proudly over the cupola of the seat of government of Mississippi," said Sgt. Osborn Oldroyd, "and if my own regiment has not had a chance to-day to cover itself with glory it has with mud."[34]

Robert Burdette of the 47th Illinois, who had seen an artillerist his own age killed right beside him, tried that evening to make sense of his baptism of fire. "I did not know—I shall never know—who shot this boy," he realized. "Nor, I think, does the man who killed him. Another boy, maybe. For there were as many schoolboys in the Confederate armies, it seemed to me, as men."[35] The potential similarities between killer and victim—and himself—haunted him. With no pen and paper available

---

32 Parrish, 3.

33 Miles, "Capture of Jackson," 3 August 1893.

34 Oldroyd, 21.

35 Burdette, 54.

to get his thoughts down, he instead wrote mental letters home—as many as a dozen of them, he later guessed. "And again I whispered a prayer, and looked up my goodnight at the stars," he remembered:

> Calm, silent, tranquil. Undimmed by the smoke of the guns. Unstained by the blood that had smeared the meadow daisies. Unshaken by all the pure tumult of charging battalions. Sweet and pure, the glittering constellations looked down upon the trampled field and the dismantled forts. Looked down upon the little world in which men lived and slept; loved and hated; fought and died. The quiet, blessed, peaceful starlight.

Yet the artillerist's death "dimmed the starlight and marred the glory of victory. . . ." Burdette laid his arm across his face to blot it out, tried not to think of "hideous and hateful things," tried instead to turn to thoughts of "love and home." Yet even as he slept and dreamed, he later said, "down through the starlight came the echo of that fainting cry under the wheels of the guns: 'Murder! Murder, boys! Oh, Murder!'"[36]

Grant, for his part, seemed to have little time for haunting introspection. Events had built up significant momentum over the previous three days, and already he began to consider his next possible moves. He had flushed Johnston from Jackson, although he had not yet eliminated Johnston as a threat, and Pemberton still lurked somewhere to the west. Other reinforcements might yet be converging on the capital.

Taking up quarters at the Bowman House, Grant convened a meeting with Sherman and McPherson, who had caught up with them to share some extraordinary

---

36 Ibid., 58-59.

news: he had intercepted a message from Johnston to Pemberton. This was the 8:40 p.m. message to Pemberton from the previous evening urging him to come up on Grant's rear. Johnston had sent the dispatch in triplicate to ensure its delivery, but one of the messengers turned out to be a Unionist, expelled months earlier from Memphis "for uttering disloyal and threatening sentiments," Grant later explained. "There was a good deal of parade about his expulsion, ostensibly as a warning to those who entertained the sentiments he expressed. . . ."[37] The exiled man finally found an opportunity to take his revenge for the indignity by giving his copy of the dispatch to McPherson.

"I was rejoiced when I learned Johnston's plans," Grant admitted, "and turned about to meet Pemberton."[38]

The battle of Champion Hill—the largest of the campaign—awaited two days away.[39]

---

37 Grant, *Memoirs*, 338-9.

38 Young, 621.

39 For the definitive account of the fight on May 16, see Timothy B. Smith, *Champion Hill: The Definitive Battle for Vicksburg* (Savas Beatie, 2006).

10

DESTRUCTION OF THE CITY

To SET his army in motion, Grant first sent word to McClernand, guarding the Federal rear: "Turn all your forces toward Bolton Station, and make all dispatch in getting there. Move troops by the most direct road from wherever they may be on the receipt of this order." He sent similar orders to Maj. Gen. Frank Blair, bringing up the supply train. Grant wanted a quick consolidation of forces that would not just reduce his own vulnerability but also let him strike at Pemberton and respond, as necessary, to Johnston—whose movements he misinterpreted. "It is evidently the design of the enemy to get north of us, and cross the Black River and beat us into Vicksburg," Grant told them. "We must not allow them to do this."[1]

With the parts of his command outside Jackson thus mobilized, and the XIII Corps shifting into position to become the army's vanguard, Grant then ordered McPherson to march the next morning back up the Clinton Road. Make for McClernand, Grant told him.

McPherson took to the task with gusto. "The enemy is still active, though defeated," he told his corps in a circular issued the night of May 14. "Let us press him and crush

---

1 See Grant to McClernand, O.R. XXIV, Pt. 3, 310 and Grant to Blair, 311.

him."² His men set out early, with the last of them rolling out of town by midmorning.

Grant chose to travel with him, expecting a fight somewhere on the road. As the headquarters staff departed the Bowman House, Lt. Col. James H. Wilson, Grant's assistant inspector general, requested a bill for the accommodations. Sixty dollars, the proprietor told him. Wilson passed the man a Confederate $100 bill. Thunderstruck, the proprietor admitted "he had expected to be paid in U.S. gold coin, or greenbacks, or the charges would have been much higher."

"Very well," Wilson countered, "charge what you please. We proposed to pay you in Confederate money." The final bill tallied up to ninety dollars.³

Sherman, meanwhile, was to stay in Jackson for an additional day "to break up railroads, to destroy the arsenal, a foundry, the cotton-factory . . . etc., etc., and then to follow McPherson."⁴ If the army was going to cripple Jackson as a transportation and manufacturing hub and remove it as a threat from Grant's rear—Grant's whole reason for capturing the city in the first place—there was much to be done. "He did the work most effectually," the army commander later praised.⁵

Grant spoke from personal observation. Before leaving town, he stopped for a final check-in with Sherman. The two took a moment to inspect a textile mill with "an immense amount of cotton, in bales, stacked outside." They decided to pop inside to take a gander. Apparently, the workers—"most of whom were girls," Grant noted—

---

2   General Orders, No. 18, McPherson, 14 May 1863, O.R. XXIV, Part 3, 312-3.

3   Cadwallader, 75.

4   Sherman, *Memoirs*, 347.

5   Grant, *Memoirs*, 338.

had not ceased operations on account of the battle the day before or for the occupation then underway. Nor did they stop when the Yankee officers entered. In fact, Grant said, their presence seemed to attract no attention at all. The two generals watched bolts of tent cloth, with "C.S.A" woven into each, roll off the looms.

I think they've done enough work, Grant finally said.

The owners, Joshua and Thomas Green, "made strong appeals based on the fact that [the factory] gave employment to very many females and poor families," Sherman recalled. Although it wove cloth for the Confederate army, the proprietors argued that its principal use was "in weaving cloth for the people." Sherman, convinced "machinery of that kind could so easily be converted into hostile uses," ignored the pleas. Any families facing want could come to Vicksburg, where the army would feed them "till they could find employment or seek refuge in some more peaceful land," Sherman decreed.[6]

Grant invited the women to gather up what cloth they could each carry and directed them out the door, and Sherman had his men put the torch to the place. "In a few minutes cotton and factory were in a blaze," Grant wrote.[7]

Elsewhere, Sherman's men carried out the work of destruction, starting with the railroads. Steele's division concentrated on the rail lines to the south and east; Tuttle's division concentrated on the north and west. "This work of destruction was well accomplished," Sherman wrote

---

6 Details from this story come from Sherman, report, 754, and Grant, *Memoirs*, 338. In his memoirs written more than twenty years after the fact, Grant places this episode at about 4:00 p.m. on May 14. Sherman, in his report, written on May 24, places it on May 15. Other evidence, such as an appeal by the Green brothers for restitution during Grant's presidency, suggests May 15, as well (see *Papers of Ulysses S. Grant*, vol. 15:608-609). President Grant, by the way, denied to support the Green brothers' claim.

7 Grant, *Memoirs*, 338.

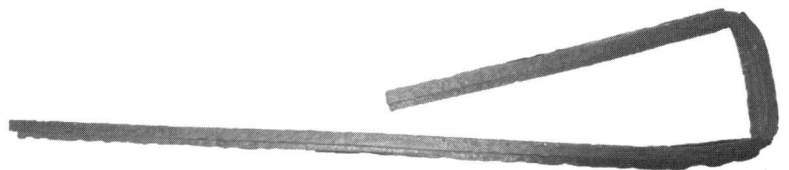

The Mississippi State Museum has on display an authentic "Sherman necktie" fished out of the Pearl River at Jackson. Note the thinness of the rail as compared to modern rails.

*Collection of the Museum Division,
Mississippi Department of Archives and History*

approvingly.[8] Wrecking crews fanned out along each line for three to four miles. "[E]very tie was burned and every rail bent, so it will require new material to put that part of the road in operation again," reported Charles Matthies.[9]

David Reed of the 12th Iowa, tasked with destroying the northern railroad toward Memphis, described the process for creating what later became infamously known as "Sherman's neckties":

> The regiment formed along the track, and, at a given signal, upset a section equal to the whole length of the regiment. The ties were then wrenched from the rails and piled up, and the rails laid across the pile. Fire was then applied to the pile, and when the rails were red-hot in the middle the ends were seized and the rail twisted [around a tree] in such manner that it could not be used again without being put through the rolling mill.[10]

Ralph Buckland's brigade, sent to destroy the railroad leading from Jackson to Vicksburg, discovered they had

8   Sherman, report, 754.

9   Matthies, O.R. XXIV, Pt. 1, 770.

10 Reed, 119.

"not a tool of any description." They borrowed four axes and trusted to luck for other tools and rations, managing to pick up five or six axes and as many picks along the way. "[A]nd with these, we commenced the work of destruction," Buckland said. Foragers went out during the day, too, bringing back "an abundance of cattle and sheep," although Buckland reported they had no bread. By nightfall, the brigade encamped about four miles from the city with a chain of pickets surrounding them and, on the 16th, continued all the way west to Clinton.[11]

To the east, Sherman's men had also been instructed to burn all the cotton and stores they could find.[12] Crews returned to the city after their day of destruction, offering one final coda. "On our return, we completely destroyed the Pearl River railroad bridge and threw the iron into the river," wrote Charles Dana Miller of the 76th Ohio.[13] Confederates had apparently already torched the wagon bridge, but that didn't stop the Federals from finishing the job. "Pearl river bridge having been burnt by the enemy, its abutments were battered down by our artillery," wrote Charles A. Willison of the 76th.[14]

The 12th Iowa, meanwhile, returned to more lighthearted duty. "We were stationed near the splendid residence of the late Brig. General [Richard] Griffith, C.S.A.," Lieutenant Reed explained, "and during the day captured nine grayback geese belonging to the forces of the said General Griffith. Their uniforms proved them

---

11 Buckland, O.R. XXIV, Pt. 1, 762-3.

12 Grant to Sherman, 14 May 1863, O.R. XXIV, Pt. 3, 312.

13 Charles Dana Miller, *The Struggle for the Life of the Republic: A Civil War Narrative by Brevet Major Charles Dana Miller, 76th Ohio Volunteer Infantry* (Kent, OH: Kent State University Press, 2004), 94.

14 Charles A. Willison, *Reminiscences of a Boy's Service with the 76th Ohio, in the Fifteenth Army Corps* (Menasha, WI: George Banta Publishing Company, 1908), 53.

DESTRUCTION OF THE CITY | 115

THE PEARL RIVER AT JACKSON

The top photo looks south at the modern railroad bridge, located in basically the same place as the wartime railroad bridge. The bottom photo looks north toward the approximate site of the wartime bridge (downtown Jackson would be to the left).

Jim Woodrick

enemies, and they were condemned to be executed." After a hard day's work, Reed was pleased to report, "Full rations of goose and enough left over for tomorrow."[15]

As some crews fanned out to wreck railroads, other crews set to work in Jackson proper destroying the state's infrastructure. "On the 15th, the ruthless hand of destruction and devastation has full sway, and immense amounts of Confederate property, military manufactories and stories are destroyed," wrote Wisconsinite S. C. Miles. Cadwallader ticked off a list: "Foundries, machine-shops, warehouses, factories, arsenals and public stores were fired as fast as flames could be kindled."[16] Sherman's men also destroyed the state arsenal, the government foundry, and the state gun carriage assembly, including the carriages for two complete six-gun batteries, stable, and carpenter and paint shops.[17] The 76th Ohio made a particularly odd find among "the novel arms to be used by the Rebels": a cache of pikes manufactured early in the war but, for whatever reason, never used or even distributed.[18] On May 18, as parts of the town still burned, a traveler observed "great numbers of pikes and pikeheads amongst the debris."[19]

Although Johnston, in his own report, had indicated the supposed evacuation of the city's supplies, a member of the 8th Wisconsin had a far different impression: "Destruction of rebel stores immense."[20]

---

15 Reed, 119. Griffith, a native of Philadelphia, had been mortally wounded on June 29, 1862, at the battle of Savage's Station during the Seven Days Battles outside Richmond.

16 Cadwallader, 74.

17 Sherman, report, 754.

18 Miller, 94.

19 Fremantle, 105.

20 Driggs, 133.

A "prison bridge" spanned the Pearl River in early 1863. Federal prisoners held there were paroled by the end of April and the prison was abandoned. Sherman's men destroyed it in May.

Harper's Weekly

Even the state penitentiary went up in flames, although not by the torch of the Federals: convicts released by Confederate authorities set fire to all the buildings of the prison, "and their lurid flames added to the holocaust everywhere prevailing. . . ."[21]

In general, Sherman did not target private property—the exception of the Greens' textile mill notwithstanding—although some collateral damage seemed unavoidable. "Mischievous soldiers" accidentally destroyed the Catholic Church and, in malice, the Confederate Hotel; neither act, Sherman said, was "justified by the rules of war," but the perpetrators could not be identified. He passed down orders to Mower to put an end to it:

21 Sherman report, 754.

"The whole town was a miserable wreck, and presented a deplorable aspect," wrote one observer in the wake of the May 15 destruction. It would be the first of several times Jackson would find itself in flames at the hands of Federal soldiers.

Harper's Weekly

It is represented to me that the provost-marshal is giving license to take the contents of stores, taking things not necessary or useful. This, if true, is wrong. Only such articles should be taken as are necessary to the subsistence of troops, and the private rights of citizens should be respected.

Please give the matter your attention. The feeling of pillage and booty will injure the morals of the troops, and bring disgrace on our cause. . . .[22]

"[M]any acts of pillage occurred that I regret," Sherman later said, blaming at least some of it on "bad rum" discovered among the town's stores.[23]

A private's-view perspective brushed off such incidents as "the evils of the circumstances of war." "[T]he guilty inhabitants are in terror," said S. C. Miles, expressing particular scorn for men and boys who were, just the day before, "in the trenches assisting in the defense of their

---

22 Sherman to Mower, 15 May 1863, O.R. XXIV, Pt. 3, 315.

23 Sherman, report, 754.

city from the despised Yankee Lincolnites. . . ."²⁴ Federals showed particular contempt for such fellows:

> their courage failed them when they saw the glittering of our bayonets, and heard the wild cheering of our advancing troops. They gave way, fled to their homes, and are this day with downcast and desponding faces, seeking protection at our hands, pleading that their property may be spared from the ruthless hand of the 'Yankee invader.'²⁵

Despite the day's destruction, said a member of the 8th Wisconsin, "the city still stands, and her magnificent capitol, with its costly and valuable records, where foul treason was first ordained, was not violated, but left unharmed as a monument of disgrace for them to reflect upon. . . ."²⁶ Fellow Wisconsinite Miles described the building as a symbol of "their outraged country's forbearance and the generosity of their hated Yankees and conquerors, a monument to [Mississippians'] shame. . . ."²⁷

And so, the saturnalia of wreckage continued into the night, but on the morning of the 16th, news arrived that changed the day. Grant alerted Sherman to the advance of Pemberton's forces and urged the XV Corps to join the rest of the army as soon as possible. Steele pulled his division out at 10 a.m., and Tuttle's followed at noon.

The men had a rag-tag look about them as they marched out of town—not as a result of the two weeks of overland campaigning so much as the plundering. "During our stay many of the soldiers, whose uniforms have become very much dilapidated and rather over-populated

---

24 Miles, "Capture of Jackson," 3 August 1893.

25 Driggs, 134.

26 Ibid, 133.

27 Miles, "Capture of Jackson," 3 August 1893.

with uncongenial inhabitants, have exchanged for any suitable article of clothing to be found in vacated stores," said Miles, "and now the troops are somewhat deficient in uniformity of dress." He admitted to appropriating new "blue-and-white pepper-and-salt denim pants and blue-gray shirt."[28]

Tobacco was also popular. "An immense amount of plug tobacco was brought out by the soldiers . . ." wrote Charles Willison, a young private with the 76th Ohio. "I think enough was left strewed over the ground at our first camp to thatch a good-sized village." Willison, for his part, had loaded himself down with seven or eight canteens full of fresh sugar he'd pillaged, although he had to abandon them along the march as the straps cut into his shoulders.[29]

Charles Miller of the 76th Ohio found time to pay a visit to the Mississippi State Library, where he "secured a few small volumes such as I could carry conveniently" before slipping out of town. He wasn't the only one with such a bibliothetic idea. Plenty of other soldiers were helping themselves to books, as well. "[I] saw a good many expensive works that I would have liked, could I have obtained the transportation," he admitted.[30]

As Sherman prepared to leave Jackson, the proprietor of the Confederate Hotel—"a very fat man," as Sherman described him—flagged the general down. *Was the hotel doomed to be burned?* the proprietor inquired. He assured Sherman that he was a law-abiding Union man. Sherman believed him: on the "Confederate Hotel" sign, he could see the words "United States" painted over but still faintly showing from beneath the word "Confederate." Sherman

---

28 Ibid.

29 Willison, 53.

30 Miller, 95.

remembered the hotel from the days before the war, when he traveled the railroad to New Orleans and the hotel served as the supper-station for the train.

But even as Sherman assured the man he "had not the least purpose" in burning the hotel, it burst into flame. "I never found out exactly who set it on fire," Sherman admitted in his memoir. Apparently, though, he wasn't the only one with memories of the hotel. He heard a report that some of his men, as prisoners of war after the battle of Shiloh, had passed through Jackson and been insulted by that same law-abiding landlord. "These men, it was said, had quietly and stealthily applied the fire underneath the hotel just as we were leaving the town," Sherman explained.[31]

Some soldiers felt bad about the damage the army had inflicted on Jackson, but few regretted it. "This ruthless destruction was necessary for the protection of our rear, as we turned to the hard task yet before us toward Vicksburg," explained Willison.[32]

Mower's brigade, acting as the provost guard, paroled all Confederate prisoners. Sherman ordered the paroles because wounded men from McPherson's corps had been left in a hospital under the care of a surgeon, Henry S. Hewitt, "to the mercy of the enemy, who I knew would re-enter Jackson as we left," he said.[33]

And indeed the Confederates did swoop right back in. Mower's brigade, as the last unit in the city, had "the rebel cavalry at its heels, as is usual with that kind of beast," said Miles, "ready to follow and hiss out their spite like a goose when one's back is turned, and still more ready to run when turned upon."[34]

31 Sherman, *Memoirs*, 347-8.

32 Willison, 52.

33 Sherman, report, 755.

34 Miles, "Capture of Jackson," 3 August 1893.

COL. JOHN CROMWELL
A member of his regiment described Col. John Cromwell thus: "Popular throughout the whole brigade, brave, generous, and handsome, he was one of the noblest of men and soldiers."

Author's collection

The last man out of the city didn't make it: Col. John N. Cromwell of the 47th Illinois.[35] The previous September, the night after the battle of Iuka, Confederates had captured Cromwell while he'd been inspecting the picket line. "Becoming lost in the darkness, he wandered into an enemy's picket and was made prisoner," a regimental historian for the 47th Illinois later recounted. "After his release he said that never again would he be taken alive, and the vow was only too well kept."[36]

As Mower's brigade withdrew from Jackson, Cromwell brought up the rear, looking for stragglers. Seeing the wounded men who were being left behind, he stopped to offer "a last word of comfort to those who would soon be prisoners as he himself had once been." As he turned to ride out of town, a company of Col. Wirt Adams's cavalry under Maj. William Yerger materialized from a side street. They shouted to Cromwell to surrender. "Half turning in

---

35 Illinois Adjutant General's Report, "47th Illinois Infantry," *Regimental and Unit Histories*, 157. https://www.cyberdriveillinois.com/departments/archives/databases/reghist.pdf (accessed 12 March 2021).

36 Cloyd Bryner, *Bugle Echoes: The Story of the Illinois 47th* (Springfield, IL: Phillips Brothers, 1905), 82.

COL. WILLIAM WIRT ADAMS

Wirt Adams, whose troopers inflicted the last casualty of the battle of Jackson, was himself buried in the city's Greenwood Cemetery following his own death in May 1888.

Library of Congress

---

his saddle, with a laugh upon his lips, he shook his head in answer and setting spurs deep in his horse's sides, sprang ahead," the Illinois historian wrote. As Cromwell made his dash for safety, Confederates gunned him down.

11

WHOSE HEARTS SHOULD BE AS BROTHERS

MILES TO the west, along the Big Black River, Pemberton was as clueless as Grant was resolute, in large part because of the communication mix-ups with Johnston and Johnston's own mysterious insincerity. Against his better judgment, the Vicksburg commander groped eastward in an attempt to catch Grant between his force and Johnston's, not knowing that Johnston was already reneging on his own plan—the responsibility for which he then tried to shift onto Pemberton. "Our being compelled to leave Jackson makes your plan impracticable," Johnston explained on May 15 from a spot ten miles northeast of the capital. He told Pemberton, "The only mode by which we can unite is your moving directly to Clinton"—a perplexing directive because Johnston was moving *away from*, not toward, that spot. Johnston was unhelpful in other ways, too. "I have no means of estimating the enemy's force at Jackson," he wrote. "The principal officers here differ very widely."[1]

Thus it was that Johnston proved his own unfitness for field service, a statement he laid out when he undertook his assignment and then spent all the subsequent days

---

1 Johnston to Pemberton, O.R. XXIV, Pt. 3, 882.

proving. What might have been a simple complaint about aches and pains, but was more probably a passive-aggressive attempt to shirk responsibility, became a self-fulfilling prophecy. "Davis knew that I had been sick five or six weeks when ordered to Mississippi," Johnston snipped defensively after the war, but in reality, his unfitness had more to do with weakness in his spine than in his physical constitution.[2] Historian Michael Ballard offered what is both an objective assessment and a damning indictment: "Johnston seldom fought if retreat was possible."[3]

Not that the Confederate president was without fault of his own. "Davis had certainly not helped by sending Johnston to take charge," argues Ballard in his Pemberton biography, "something Johnston never did or had any desire to do."[4] Caught between the clashing egos and conflicting orders of Davis and Johnston, and pinned beneath the weight of negative public opinion, it's little wonder Pemberton (a "defeated and disheartened general" by this point, says Ballard) managed to live down to expectations despite his best efforts and loyal intentions.[5] His worst days of the campaign, and his ultimate ignominy, were still to come.

For Grant, the fall of Jackson proved to be an important operational victory. By shooing away Johnston mere hours after the Confederate commander's boots hit the ground, Grant removed a threat from his rear, allowing him to fully concentrate on the out-matched Pemberton.

---

2   Johnston, *B&L*, 479.

3   Ballard, *Pemberton*, 158.

4   Ibid, 156.

5   Ibid.

"It is difficult to overestimate the importance of Grant's capture of Jackson," says historian Timothy B. Smith.[6] Ed Bearss, passing judgment on the episode, agrees:

> The Jackson engagement . . . was of major significance to Grant . . . [B]y capturing Jackson [Grant] scattered what within another 24 hours would have become a formidable force. Such an army in possession of Jackson and with the railroads passing through the city facilitating its reinforcement, and being commanded by the popular Johnston, could have constituted a terrible threat to Grant's army, dependent as it was for reinforcements of men and military hardware on a dirt road linking it to the Grand Gulf enclave.[7]

Instead, points out Smith, "The Confederate situation in Mississippi worsened considerably with the evacuation and loss of Jackson. . . ."[8]

Although the specter of Johnston would lurk behind the Federals for weeks, the threat never materialized, and Grant eventually realized it probably never would. Johnston would remain distant throughout the rest of Grant's Vicksburg campaign, and only make a tepid approach toward the Big Black River and Vicksburg too little, too late.

Following the fall of the Hill City on July 4, Sherman would finally shoo Johnston away for good by July 16—ironically, again at Jackson. Johnston holed up in the city and, beginning July 10, Sherman laid siege. Johnston pulled out and Jackson fell on July 16—and thus ended Johnston's adventures in Mississippi. For good measure,

---

6   Smith, *Champion Hill*, 102.

7   Bearss, *The Campaign for Vicksburg*, 554.

8   Smith, *Champion Hill*, 103.

Despite the destruction wrought upon Jackson on May 14-15, the city got off comparatively easy. Later Federal visits to the city would leave the capital in much worse shape, thus inspiring the name "Chimneyville." This view of the Old Capitol includes ruins of the Bowman House hotel in the foreground.

Mississippi Department of Archives and History

Sherman torched the city again, so badly that people called it "Chimneyville" because that's all that seemed to remain.[9]

Sherman passed through Jackson yet again in February 1864 as part of the Meridian campaign. "A new burning has been inflicted on this afflicted town," he wrote his wife.[10]

9   For the definitive account of the siege of Jackson, see James Woodrick, *The Civil War Siege of Jackson, Mississippi* (History Press, 2016).

10 Sherman to Ellen Sherman, 7 February 1864, *Sherman's Civil War: Selected Correspondence of William T. Sherman, 1860-1865*, Brooks D. Simpson and Jean V. Berlin, eds. (Chapel Hill, NC: University of North Carolina Press, 1999), 602.

A reproduction "Sherman necktie" is on display—wrapped around a tree stump—outside the museum in Meridian, Mississippi. Sherman pushed through Jackson on his way to Meridian in February 1864.

Chris Mackowski

The loss of the state capital on May 14 was a blow to southern morale. It threw "a damper over the spirits of the people," said Pettus's secretary, James Rives.[11] The Montgomery, Alabama, *Daily Mail* referred to it as a "serious disaster."[12] John B. Jones, a clerk in the Confederate War Department in far-off Richmond, wrote, "This is a dark cloud over the hopes of patriots, for

---

11 Rives to Pettus, 15 May 1863, in Governor's Correspondence, Vol. LVL, quoted in Dubay, 174.

12 Quoted in the *Montgomery* (AL) *Daily Mail*, 15 May 1863, 2.

Vicksburg is seriously endangered."[13] (Jones's diary entry for May 14 was, incidentally, preceded by days of entries about the fall and funeral of a different Jackson, Lt. Gen. Thomas "Stonewall" Jackson, mortally wounded on May 2 during the battle of Chancellorsville.) Jones went on to say the fall of Vicksburg "would be the worst blow we have yet received," illustrating a larger historical point: Jackson's fall was overshadowed at the time and in memory by the threat to, and eventual fall of, Vicksburg.

Johnston encouraged that historical amnesia, too. In his fabulously defensive memoir, he criticized the official Federal report for blowing the encounter out of proportion. "[T]heir skirmishing with Gregg's and Walker's brigades is exaggerated into a heavy engagement of two hours, in which the Confederate main body was badly beaten and pursued until night," Johnston scoffed. "On the contrary, the skirmishing was trifling, and there was nothing like pursuit—into Jackson even."[14] His performance during the Vicksburg campaign was the nadir of his career, and the loss of a state capital was a particular smudge, so it's little wonder Johnston poo-pooed the episode and wanted it forgotten. His strange brush-off of the city's defense on May 14 only indicts him worse.

In taking the capital, Grant demonstrated that he could come into Jefferson Davis's home and pretty much move with impunity, even taking the seat of its fire-eating government. Jackson became the third Confederate state capital to fall, following Nashville and Baton Rouge. "In some ears it would sound like a very big thing for a Yankee army to occupy the capital of the great secession state of Mississippi, and home of the President of the

---

13 J. B. Jones, *A Rebel War Clerk's Diary*, vol. 1 (Philadelphia: J. B. Lippincott & Co., 1866), 324. With thanks to Dwight Hughes for helping me track this down.

14 Joseph E. Johnston, 177.

Southern Confederacy," observed Albert Theodore Goodloe, a veteran of the 35th Alabama, years later. Goodloe supposed Grant actually had "no particular use for Jackson, only for the enhancement of his own greatness, the *hallelujah* effect it would certainly produce in the military and civil domain of Abe Lincoln, and the possibly depressing impression it would make upon our armies and the people of the South generally."[15]

If it created a depressing impression for Confederates, the capture of Jackson had quite the opposite effect on Federals, boosting their already high morale as they operated deep in the heart of hostile territory. You are "heroes in American history," James McPherson told his men, and they believed it.[16] The successful crossing of the river, the victories at Port Gibson and Raymond, the fall of Grand Gulf, the conquering of the state capital—this accumulated record of success would do much to influence the men's mindset even as they knew they biggest challenge of the campaign, the capture of Vicksburg, still lay before them. "Not a soldier in this army but realized the important mission of our great leader," wrote Charles Dana Miller of the 76th Ohio. "Work was done with willing hand and the marches were with elastic steps."[17]

For all its operational usefulness to Grant, though, the battle of Jackson was not a turning point in the campaign the way the fall of Grand Gulf or the victory at Raymond were—where Grant changed his plans on the fly based on the outcomes—and it didn't have the magnitude of Champion Hill, yet to be fought on May 16. The significance

---

15 Albert Theodore Goodloe, *Confederate Echoes: A Voice from the South in the Days of Secession and of the Southern Confederacy* (Nashville: M. E. Church, South, Smith & Lamar, 1907), 275-6.

16 General Orders No. 18, McPherson, O.R. XXIV, Pt. 3, 312-3.

17 Miller, 94.

of the battle of Jackson actually rested in the "might have beens" averted by Grant's success: What if Johnston had not abandoned Jackson, which had thrown away his strategic advantage? What if he had concentrated Confederate reinforcements? What if he had acted more aggressively? What if he acted in a way consistent with his own orders to Pemberton?

By the time Vicksburg fell, the battle at Jackson looked like a rather minor affair. Gabriel Bouck, colonel of the 18th Wisconsin, offered a summary that reflected the fight's succinctness: "Gave them battle and whipped them."[18]

According the McPherson's official report—the only cumulative tally submitted on either side—Confederates suffered some 845 casualties and the stinging loss of 17 guns. Federals, in comparison, suffered exactly 300 casualties in all, 265 of them along the Clinton Road.[19] The 17th Iowa—"hotly engaged," said Colonel Hillis—bore the brunt of those Federal losses: 16 killed, 60 wounded, 1 disabled by a shell, 3 missing for a total of 80 men out of 350 engaged—23 percent of the regiment and 27 percent of Grant's total losses.[20]

In the immediate aftermath of the fight, Sgt. Osborn H. Oldroyd of the 20th Ohio had the chance to walk across the battlefield. His unit, part of Maj. Gen. John Logan's division, did not see much action, but they did see its consequences.

18 Bouck, O.R. XXIV, Pt. 1, 773.

19 McPherson, O.R. XXIV, Pt. 1, 639. "Confederate casualty figures, as usual, are very difficult to determine," says historian Jim Woodrick, who points out, "845 would be an enormously high percentage." Gist's official report lists 198 casualties, for instance. Add up the Confederate casualties mentioned in Union reports on both flanks, and Jim sees issues with McPherson's math. "I can't see where—even inflating numbers a bit—Confederate losses could have been much more than 300, K/W/M, with the loss of 17 guns." McPherson's larger number may include captured civilians still manning the trenches when the Confederate army left.

20 Hollis, 779.

132 | The Battle of Jackson, Mississippi

One of the bronze tableaus on the Iowa state memorial at Vicksburg depicts the charge by the 17th Iowa at the battle of Jackson. Sculpted by H. H. Kitson, the memorial was dedicated on November 15, 1906, although construction didn't wrap up until 1912—at a cost of $100,000.

Chris Mackowski

As the Ohioans marched toward the city, they traveled the Clinton Road as it passed through the Wright farmstead. Dead and wounded members of the 24th South Carolina lay scatted around the farmhouse and hedge fence where Crocker's division clashed with Colquitt.

"I shall not forget the conversation I have had with a wounded rebel," Oldroyd wrote in his diary:

> He said that his regiment last night was full of men who had never before met us, and who felt sure it would be easy to whips us. How they were deceived! He said part of his regiment was behind a hedge fence, where they felt

comparatively safe, but the Yankees jumped right over without stopping, and swept everything before them.

I never saw finer looking men than the killed and wounded rebels of to-day, and with the smooth face of him, lying in a garden mortally wounded, I was so taken, that I eased his thirst with a drink from my own canteen. His piteous glance at me at that time I shall never forget.

It is on the battlefield and among the dead and dying we get to know each other better—nay, even our own selves. Administering to a stranger, we think of his mother's love, as dear to him as our own to us. When the fight is over, away all bitterness. Let us leave with the foe some tokens of good will, that, when the cruel war at last is over, may be kindly remembered.

I trust our enemies may yet be led to hail in good faith the return of peace and the restoration of the Union. This is a domestic war, the saddest of all, being fought between those whose hearts should be as brothers; and when it is at an end, may those hearts again throb together beneath the folds of the flag that once waved for defence over their sires and themselves—a flag whose proud motto will be, "peace on earth and good will to men."[21]

21 Oldroyd, 21.

134 | THE BATTLE OF JACKSON, MISSISSIPPI

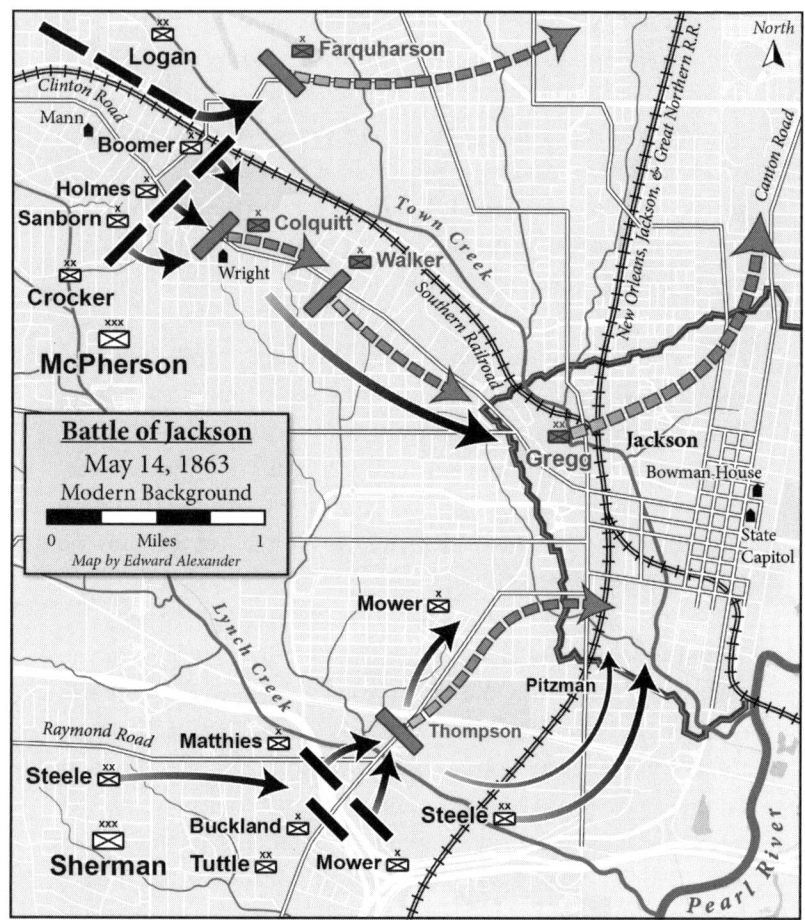

BATTLE OF JACKSON (MODERN BACKGROUND)

This map illustrates the two-front action of the battle of Jackson laid out on a background of the modern city for reference. Development has swallowed the battlefield, but the city of Jackson still has plenty of Civil War history to explore.

Edward Alexander

12

The Jackson Battlefield

JIM WOODRICK waits for me on the steps of a building that's almost aggressive in its blockiness. Opened in 2003, the William F. Winter Archives and History Building manages to exude "classical government gravitas" with its white granite façade and tall narrow windows, while also somehow looking like a Soviet-era rectangular-block throwback. Jim rises and greets me with a smile and handshake. While Facebook acquaintances, we've never meet in person before, but Jim shows me all the gentle kindness of an old country doctor. He has graciously agreed to show me the Civil War sites of Jackson—or what's left of them.

The Winter building is one of two offices operated by the Mississippi Department of Archives and History (MDAH); Jim, a 24-year veteran of the department, worked in the other, the Capers building, just a couple blocks away on the far side of the Old Capitol Museum. Founded in 1902, the department is, itself, an important result of the Civil War. "In the 1890s Mississippi experienced an economic and educational revitalization that sparked an interest in preserving and promoting the 'Southern identity,' including its historical records, particularly those relating to the recent Civil War," say historians Lisa Speer and Heather Mitchell. "Taking a proactive role in

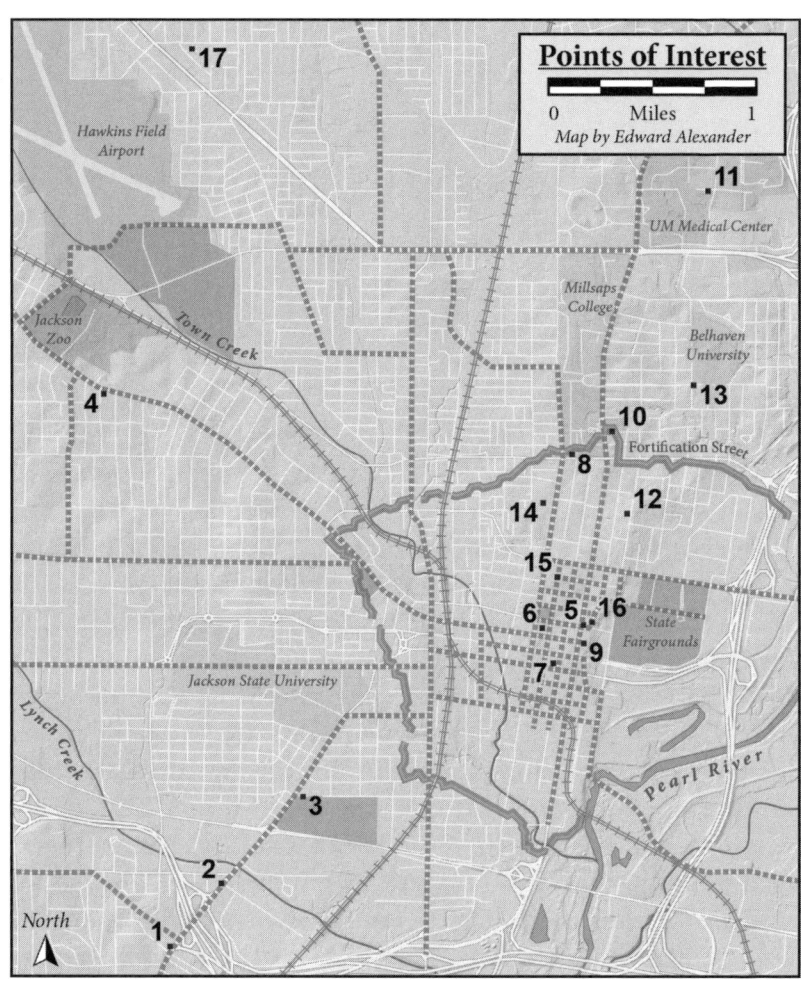

POINTS OF INTEREST

Sites Related to the Battle of Jackson
1) Sherman's Approach
2) Battlefield Shopping Center
3) Battlefield Park
4) Wright House site
5) Bowman House site
6) Governor's Mansion
7) Jackson City Hall
8) Manship House
9) Old Capitol Museum

Additional Points of Interest
10) "Cotton Bale" Battery
11) Union Earthworks
12) Oaks House Museum
13) Welty House Museum
14) Greenwood Cemetery
15) Mississippi State Capitol
16) Two Mississippi Museums
17) Medgar and Myrlie Evers National Historic Site

the preservation of these important records would ensure that scholarship reflected the South's position on such complex and contested issues as slavery and secession."[1]

As I will discover over the course of my time exploring the Vicksburg campaign, the MDAH has done incredible work preserving Civil War history in the state. Jim, during his tenure with the department, served as its unofficial "Civil War guy," playing an important role in conservation, preservation, and interpretation efforts. To his credit, he always speaks of those efforts in first-person plural—"we" did this and "we" did that—highlighting the team nature of the work.

Jackson has a population just shy of 155,000, making it the largest city in Mississippi. Jim knows his way around and so offers to drive. We climb into his white Ford Escape and begin to connect the dots of Jackson's Civil War story. Alas, they don't tell a very complete picture because the city has grown so dramatically since the 1860s, swallowing almost every physical trace of the war.

What follows is a list of sites related to the May 1863 battle of Jackson. Because the battle took place on two fronts, they city's layout makes it impractical to string together a chronologically logical tour. Therefore, the map lays out locations and the text explains what's there without offering specific directions on getting from one spot to the next. Travelers should use caution while driving in city traffic.

I also call attention here to several other points of interest, including a few that relate the July 1863 siege of Jackson. For a comprehensive treatment of that action, I refer you to Jim's excellent *The Civil War Siege of Jackson, Mississippi* (History Press, 2016).

---

1 Lisa Speer and Heather Mitchell, "'The Mississippi Plan': Dunbar Rowland and the Creation of the Mississippi Department of Archives and History," *Provenance, Journal of the Society of Georgia Archivists* 22 no. 1 (2004), 52, 53. https://digitalcommons.kennesaw.edu/provenance/vol22/iss1/5 (accessed 16 March 2022).

Sherman's Approach
The Corner of Carmel Avenue and Terry Road

At the corner of Carmel Avenue and Terry Road, a small dead-end paved way parallels Terry. Jim pulls in and parks the car, and we walk back out to the busy edge of Terry Road. We stand next to the southbound lane looking north.

From here, we can see a modern version of what the men of William T. Sherman's XV Corps saw as they advanced from Raymond toward the outskirts of Jackson. I have to erase from my view a highway overpass and the urban sprawl as I look toward downtown Jackson in the distance. Of course, there would have been no high-rise buildings in 1863, but as Jim points out, those same downtown buildings today provide a good point of reference for understanding how far out of town Sherman's men still were when they finally bumped into Confederate resistance.

The vantage point along Terry Road also offers a good understanding of the general topography of the battlefield, which has otherwise been lost to development. Terry Road descends along a still-visible slope toward Lynch Creek (not visible from this position). On the far side of the creek, Albert Thompson's Confederate forces awaited.

Battlefield Shopping Center
1817 Terry Road

The name "Battlefield Shopping Center" is the only remaining testament to the otherwise lost battlefield of May 14, 1863. Standing in the parking lot, facing Terry

Road (top photo), a visitor can orient oneself to the action as it unfolded: Sherman's XV Corps approached from the right, coming down the hill that's now on the far side of the highway overpass. They would have deployed coming down the hill and across the ground on either side of the road in this area.

Meanwhile, Confederates first arrayed to the left of this position (bottom photo) on the far side of Lynch Creek. Confederate artillery would have been somewhere as far back as Battlefield Park, about three-tenths of a mile to the northeast of the shopping center parking lot.

The bridge over Lynch Creek, one-tenth of a mile to the northeast, is visible from the shopping center parking lot, but the creek itself is difficult to see. It's worth finding a spot to take a peek at the creek (using extreme caution because of the traffic). The steep banks make it readily apparent why Sherman's men had to secure the bridge at all costs: with the pouring rain, the creek was swollen in its banks, making it impossible to ford (see the photo on page 80).

As Sherman's men forced a crossing of the bridge, "Task Force Thompson" retreated from the ground on the far side of the creek. They moved northeast along modern Terry Road (which turns into University Boulevard), heading toward the fortifications that ringed the town.

Battlefield Park
953 West Porter Street

At 54 acres, Battlefield Park between Porter Street, University Blvd., and U.S. 80 is the oldest and largest park in the city of Jackson. Established in 1927, the park boasts basketball and tennis courts, a playground, and a picnic area and pavilion and is often the scene of robust use during the day; however, the park's reputation has

The Jackson Battlefield | 141

been marred over the years by crime. "Battlefield Park fights for its reputation," a 2015 newspaper headline declared—a story that seems to remain true.[2] On my first visit to Jackson in May 2015, a body had been found in the park just days earlier, with two others found there the preceding January. As I prepped for my August 2021 trip, I read that a man had been found on March 31, 2021, at 11 a.m., shot to death in the park's play area.[3] This is all to say: use caution when visiting the park, and do so only during the day.

However, Battlefield Park offers one of the few undeveloped spots where a visitor can walk the ground where part of the battle of Jackson took place. From this area, Confederate artillery deployed as part of "Task Force Thompson" opened fire on William T. Sherman's

2 R. L. Nave, "Battlefield Park Fights For Its Reputation," Jackson Free Press, 28 January 2015. https://www.jacksonfreepress.com/news/2015/jan/28/battlefield-park-fights-its-reputation/.

3 Rosyln Anderson, "Jackson body count mounts with discovery of shooting victim in Battlefield Park," Jackson Free Press, 31 March 2021. https://www.wlbt.com/2021/03/31/jackson-body-count-mounts-with-discovery-shooting-victim-battlefield-park/.

advancing XV Corps on May 14, 1863. To mark the spot, two decrepitly skeletal artillery pieces that date back to the Spanish-American War-era sit behind a shin-high line of earthworks. A squat monument erected by the United Daughters of the Confederacy tries to suggest additional gravitas.

A nearby sign offers context:

This park and the surrounding area was involved in the Civil War action which occurred in Jackson on May 14, 1863, and July 9-17, 1863. The earthworks here constitute the most tangible remains of the extensive fortifications which were erected around the city. The property was acquired by the city of Jackson in 1927.

In fact, the works are left over from Sherman's investiture of the city in July following the fall of Vicksburg, NOT part of the "extensive fortifications" erected around the city prior to the May battle.

"So," Jim tells me, "other than identifying the trenches as Confederate, and pointing the guns in the wrong direction, and the guns being from the wrong war—the UDC ladies got everything right." As best as he's been able to tell, the UDC created their interpretation, as well-meaning as it might have been, "out of thin air."

THE JACKSON BATTLEFIELD | 143

O. P. Wright House Site
southeast corner of West Capitol and Delaware streets

The O. P. Wright house once stood on what is now a trash-strewn empty lot. West Capitol Street, which took us to the spot, was pock-marked with massive potholes and lined with vacant shops and spray-painted buildings. Fortunately, the topography of the one-time battlefield was still visible through the urban blight. The Wright house once stood along the crest of a ridge; on the northwest side, West Capitol Street descended a slope as it pointed onward toward the Jackson Zoo and, five miles beyond, Clinton. James McPherson's XVII Corps would have approached Jackson from that direction.

Bowman House Site
southeast corner of East Amite Street and North Street

The five-story Bowman House hotel, built in 1857, stood on the corner across from where the Mississippi Department of Archives and History now stands. That

location put the hotel in close proximity to the state capitol (now the Old Capitol Museum), making it a hub of political activity. On May 14, the hotel had the distinction of serving as the headquarters (at different times) for both Joseph E. Johnston and Ulysses S. Grant. The hotel survived the May battle but burned down on June 9, 1863.

Governor's Mansion
300 East Capitol Street

The Mississippi governor's mansion stands regal in its antebellum splendor, which dates back to 1842. Tours of the mansion are available on a limited basis.

At the end of the July siege, Sherman commandeered the governor's mansion. "Last night, at the Governor's Mansion, in Jackson, we had a beautiful supper and union of the generals of this army," he wrote on July 19.[4]

---

4   Sherman to David Porter, 19 July 1863, Official Records of the Union and Confederate Navies in the War of the Rebellion, Vol. 25, 314.

Sherman noted in that same letter that "State house, governor's mansion, and some fine dwellings, well within the lines of intrenchment, remain untouched," but otherwise, "Jackson, once the pride and boast of Mississippi, is now a ruined town." Sherman also noted that the westward-stretching ten-mile break in the railroad his men had made in May remained untouched, "so that Jackson ceases to be a place for the enemy to collect stores and men from which to threaten our great river [the Mississippi]." With apparent satisfaction, he observed, "the good folks of Jackson will not soon again hear the favorite locomotive whistle."

Jackson City Hall
219 South President Street

It's little wonder historian Steven Woodworth speculated that some Union soldiers may have mistaken the Jackson City Hall for the Mississippi Capitol. With four Doric columns in front, each rising three stories tall, the structure looks imposing. The building originally had

a domed top, removed in 1874, which added to its capitol-doppelganger aura.

An original city hall was built on the spot in 1847, but by 1853, due to some kind of "structural failure," the building was razed and a new one was built in its place.[5] ("That's what you get from the lowest bidder," I thought to myself). The building underwent a twentieth-century refurbishment in 1963.

Legend has it that Sherman, a Mason, spared the building from destruction because it contained a Masonic Lodge (it contained an Oddfellows Lodge, too) and designated it for use as a hospital, instead. Jim tells me the oft-repeated tale about the Lodge is highly unlikely, though. "I've found little evidence to support it," he says.

---

5 "Historic Resources Inventory Fact Sheet," Mississippi Department of Archives and History https://www.apps.mdah.ms.gov/Public/prop.aspx?id=11810&view=facts&y=738 (accessed 3 March 2022).

Manship House
420 East Fortification Street

In a city full of Greek Revival mansions, Charles Henry Manship's Gothic revival "cottage villa" stands out. With its ornamental trim along the eaves and porches, I think it looks like a gingerbread house.

Manship came to Jackson from his native Maryland in the 1830s, attracted by the city's building boom. He pitched in on the original state capitol, a project that symbolized his later marriage of professional and political interests. Manship opened a shop in town that sold paint and wallpaper; he also worked as a city clerk and as postmaster. Eventually, he became an alderman, and in 1862 and 1863, he served as mayor.

When Grant's army arrived in May 1863, Manship skipped town. In his absence, Confederate Brig. Gen. John Adams used Manship's house as a temporary headquarters as he helped coordinate the city's defenses. After Grant left, Manship returned and was there for Sherman's visit in July where he was forced to surrender the city after Joe Johnston skipped town.

Manship's house, built in 1857 on a four-acre lot on the outskirts of town, is "unpretentious but spacious," says the MDAH. Manship and his wife, Adaline, had fifteen children, ten of whom reached adulthood.

"Although the city has grown up around the house, it stands in its original setting of native trees and shrubs, some of which may have been planted by Manship himself," the MDAH says.[6]

Old Capitol Museum
100 State Street

"When it was built in 1839, the massive limestone exterior, copper dome, and grand interior spaces made the Old Capitol the most distinguished building in

---

6 https://www.mdah.ms.gov/explore-mississippi/manship-house-museum (accessed 3 March 2022).

Mississippi," says the MDAH, which still touts the Old Capitol as the state's "most historic building."[7]

Some of that history included the 1839 Married Women's Property Act, which allowed women to legally own personal property and real estate; the state's Articles of Secession, passed on January 9, 1861; and state constitutions passed in 1868 and 1890.

Following the completion of the new capitol in 1903, the building housed state offices until 1959. It then underwent renovation and, in 1961, reopened as the state museum. Hurricane Katrina damaged the building in 2005; it reopened again in 2009. From 2019-2022, the building underwent an additional $2.6 million restoration, focusing on the copper dome, windows, and interior plaster.

On the south side of the Old Capitol sits the Charlotte Capers Archives and History Building—Jim's home office when he still worked for MDAH. In front of the building stands the state's impressive Confederate monument,

---

7   https://www.mdah.ms.gov/explore-mississippi/old-capitol-museum (accessed 3 March 2022).

built in 1891 in the middle of a nice open lawn on the capitol grounds once designated as "Confederate Park." Apparently, the Capers building was intentionally built right up almost against the monument. They're so close that if the two were walking down the street and the monument stopped, the Capers building would blunder right into the monument's backside.

The monument features a sarcophagal room for a base, with a tall spire rising above and a solider at rest-arms standing vigil atop. Inside the room, a marble statue of Jefferson Davis, carved in Italy and brought to Mississippi, looks out from behind iron bars and a plexiglass wall. *It's Fort Monroe all over again*, I think. Jim explains that the space used to be open, but vandals kept defacing the statue. Davis was originally moved into the Old Capitol, but after Hurricane Katrina damaged the building, the statue came back outside and was locked up for its own protection.

Other Points of Interest

"Cotton Bale" Battery—*Manship Street*

Here, in July 1863, a portion of the city's defenses jutted outward as a salient. A sign, erected in 2007 by the MDAH, marks the spot along Manship Street east of North State Street. Once upon a time, the position would have looked out from a high bluff, but a highrise towers in front of us now, blocking any view. On the morning of July 17, a black man waved a white flag from the Cotton Bale Battery, alerting Federals to Joe Johnston's withdrawal (his second abandonment of the city in two months, nearly to the day). Federals soon flooded into the city.

Greenwood Cemetery—*George Street*

According to the MDAH, Greenwood Cemetery is the oldest landmark in Jackson, authorized by the Mississippi Legislature on January 1, 1823. Six Confederate generals are buried there, including Brig. Gen. William Barksdale, mortally wounded at Gettysburg on July 2, 1863, and cavalryman Brig. Gen. William Wirt Adams (below), whose men fired the last shots of the battle of Jackson. The cemetery also has a historic marker denoting "Confederate burial ground" (above): "Over 450 Confederate soldiers who died in and around Jackson during the Civil War are buried here. Their names are known but not the exact site of each grave, as some were reburied here from graves where they fell."

Medgar and Myrlie Evers Home National Monument—
2332 Margaret Walker Alexander Drive

While not a Civil War-related site, I nonetheless found Medgar and Myrlie Evers home one of the most poignant spots to visit in Jackson. It also serves as an important story in the thread "From Civil War to Civil Rights."

Built in 1956 and, since November 2020, operated by the National Park Service as a national historic site, the Medgar and Myrlie Evers home sits in a quiet suburban neighborhood that might still be hunkered in the mid-1960s somewhere. Evers was a field secretary for the NAACP—the first in Mississippi—and spent his time relentlessly organizing voter registration drives, commercial boycotts, vigil services, and other acts of nonviolent protest.

Evers was assasinated in his own driveway on June 12, 1963. As a World War Two veteran, he received a burial with full military honors at Arlington National Cemetery.

Mississippi State Capitol—*Fronting Mississippi Street, between N. President and N. West streets*

Built in 1903, Mississippi's Capitol doesn't feature in the city's Civil War story. It does, however, feature an impressive "Monument to the Women of the Confederacy" on the grounds directly in front of the building. Sculpted by Belle Kinney for the United Confederate Veterans, the monument depicts the central figure of Fame laying a wreath on the head of a woman as she comforts a dying Confederate soldier. Inscriptions on the sides of the monument honor "our mothers," "our daughters," "our sisters," and "our wives." The cornerstone was laid on June 3, 1912—the birthday of Mississippi native Jefferson Davis, who is quoted on the front of the monument.

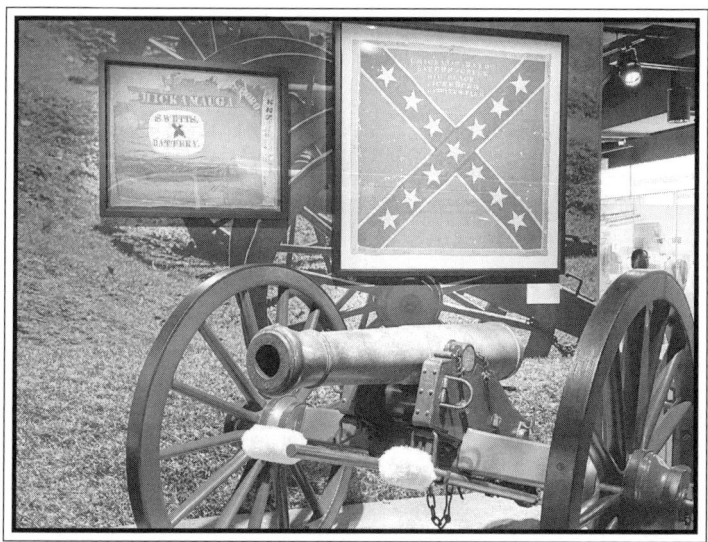

Museum of Mississippi History and Mississippi Civil Rights Museum—*222 North Street*

Collectively known (and marketed) as Two Mississippi Museums, this two-for-one museum experience operated by the MDAH is phenomenal.

On the "Mississippi History" side, Civil War travelers will find a good collection of artifacts that cover not only the military but also the civilian wartime experience, highlighted by an outstanding collection of Civil War flags.

On the "Mississippi Civil Rights" side, a vestibule exhibit sets the stage by introducing slavery and recapping the war, with a particular emphasis on events in the Magnolia State. From there, the first gallery is focused on Reconstruction and its aftermath. Successive galleries bring the story forward to the present, with displays on Emmett Till, desegregation, the Freedom Riders, the assassination of Medgar Evers, sit-ins, and other pivotal events. It was one of the most powerful and effective museum experiences I've ever had.

Oaks House Museum—*823 N. Jefferson Street*

Built circa 1853, the Boyd House, known as "The Oaks," is a Greek Revival-style cottage. Four-time mayor James Hervey Boyd lived in the house with his wife, Eliza, and their six kids. In 1863, when Federals came a-knocking in May and in July, Boyd was between gigs as mayor and instead was serving as a city alderman. Boyd's house survived the various burnings of Jackson, making it now one of the city's oldest dwellings.

Union Earthworks—*University Drive*

Once the site of the Mississippi insane asylum, the University of Mississippi Medical Center now surrounds one of the last physical remnants of Jackson's Civil War landscape: an artillery lunette erected  by John G. Parke's IX Corps as part of the siege of Jackson. "On July 11-14," says the state historical marker on the site, "the six guns of Batteries L and M, 3rd U.S. Artillery, fired 257 rounds into the city and its defenses."

Welty House—*1109 Pinehurst Street*

Mississippi admirably venerates its authors. One of the towering figures in the state's literary tradition was Jackson native Eudora Welty (1909-2001). Welty won, among other awards, the 1973 Pulitzer Prize for Fiction and the Presidential Medal of Freedom.

Best known for writing about the South, Welty nonetheless only wrote one piece about the Civil War, a short story called "The Burning." Welty considered the story—published in *Harper's* in 1951—"such a dark old one" and expressed a lot of ambivalence about it. "I abominate the Civil War and everything about it," she once told an interviewer, "and I don't feel anything but horror and infinite regret, even just despair sometimes that it happened. I mean, despair over the tremendous loss of life. . . ."[8]

Welty's house sits in a historic neighborhood called Bellhaven. According to the MDAH:

> The Belhaven neighborhood developed north of the city as Jackson's first suburb. Composed of more than 1,300 historic structures dating from as early as 1904, Belhaven is Mississippi's largest historic district. The neighborhood includes a wide variety of building styles with a mixture of commercial and residential developments, as well as religious and educational institutions. The Belhaven Historic District is listed in the National Register of Historic Places.

Also in the Belhaven neighborhood, on the northwest corner of the intersection of Greymont Avenue and Poplar Boulevard—about two-tenths of a mile from Eudora Welty's home—stands a historical marker chronicling the "Charge of the 2nd Michigan." "This is one I helped get up," Jim tells me as we stop to read the marker. Through his efforts, MDAH erected the sign in 2017 to tell a story from Sherman's siege of the city:

---

8 Quoted in Susan V. Donaldson, "Was 'The Burning' the Hardest Story for Eudora Welty To Write?: Disavowing the Rituals of the American Civil War," *Literary Hub*, 4 February 2020, https://lithub.com/was-the-burning-the-hardest-story-for-eudora-welty-to-write/ (accessed 3 March 2022).

The Jackson Battlefield

During the Civil War siege of Jackson, on July 11, 1863, Union soldiers in the 2nd Michigan Infantry staged an impromptu assault on the city's fortifications. Advancing south through what is today eastern Belhaven, they overran a campsite north of the earthworks and struck the main Confederate line positioned along the heights south of Fortification Street. Though heavily outnumbered, the Michiganders fought to within 200 yards of the fortified ridge before Col. William Humphrey gave the order to retire.

The Michiganders' axis of advance took them to the east of the Cotton Bale Battery, which was well positioned to pour enfilading fire on them. Fortification Street today marks the course of the city's defenses erected in May and defended again in July 1863.

Order of Battle

Union Forces
(forces engaged)

Army of the Tennessee
Maj. Gen. Ulysses S. Grant

XV CORPS: Maj. Gen. William T. Sherman
THIRD DIVISION: Brig. Gen. James M. Tuttle

First Brigade: Brig. Gen. Ralph P. Buckland
114th Illinois · 93rd Indiana · 72nd Ohio · 95th Ohio

Second Brigade: Brig. Gen. Joseph A. Mower
*47th Illinois · 5th Minnesota · 11th Missouri
8th Wisconsin*

Third Brigade: Brig. Gen. Charles L. Matthies
8th Iowa · 12th Iowa · 35th Iowa

Artillery: Capt. Nelson T. Spoor
*2nd Iowa Battery (6 guns)
1st Illinois Light Artillery, Company E (6 guns)*

Cavalry: Lt. Col. Simeon D. Swan

XVII CORPS: Maj. Gen. James B. McPherson
SEVENTH DIVISION: Brig. Gen. Marcellus M. Crocker

First Brigade: Col. John B. Sanborn
*48th Indiana · 59th Indiana · 4th Minnesota
18th Wisconsin*

Second Brigade: Col. Samuel A. Holmes
17th Iowa · 10th Missouri · 24th Missouri · 80th Ohio

Third Brigade: Col. George B. Boomer
93rd Illinois · 5th Iowa · 10th Iowa · 26th Missouri

Artillery: Capt. Franks C. Sands
1st Missouri Light Artillery, Company M (4 guns)
6th Wisconsin Light Artillery (6 guns)

Cavalry:
6th Missouri Cavalry: Col. C. Wright
Provision Cavalry Battalion: Capt. J. S. Foster
2nd Illinois, Companies A & E · 4th Missouri, Company F
4th Independent Company, Ohio Cavalry

Confederate Forces

Departments of Tennessee and Mississippi
Gen. Joseph E. Johnston

Field Commander of Troops Engaged
Brig. Gen. John Gregg

Gregg's Brigade: Col. Robert Farquharson
3rd Tennessee · 10th and 30th Tennessee (consolidated)
41st Tennessee · 50th Tennessee
1st Tennessee Battalion · 7th Texas Infantry

Artillery: Capt. Hiram M. Bledsoe
Bledsoe's Missouri Battery (2 guns)

Gist's Brigade: Col. Peyton H. Colquitt
46th Georgia · 14th Mississippi · 24th South Carolina

Artillery: Capt. James A. Hoskins
Brookhaven Light Artillery (4 guns)

Walker's Brigade: Brig. Gen. W. H. T. Walker
30th Georgia · 1st Georgia Sharpshooter Battalion
4th Louisiana Battalion

Artillery: Capt. Robert Martin
Martin's Georgia Battery (4 guns)

Miscellaneous
3rd Kentucky Mounted Infantry ("Task Force Thompson")
Independent Company, Georgia Cavalry
1st Battalion, Mississippi State Militia

SOURCES

The War of the Rebellion: A Compilation of the Official Records of the Union and Confederate Armies (Washington, D.C.: Government Printing Office, 1889), Series I and IV.

Avalon Project, Yale Law School
Papers of Jefferson Davis, Rice University
Papers of Ulysses S. Grant
Vicksburg National Military Park archives
Wisconsin Historical Society

Jackson (MS) *Clarion*
Jackson (MS) *Free Press*
Memphis (TN) *Appeal*
Mobile (AL) *Daily Advertiser and Register*
Montgomery (AL) *Daily Mail*
National Tribune

Primary

Flavel C. Barber, *Holding the Line: The Third Tennessee Infantry, 1861-1864*, Robert H. Ferrell, ed. (Kent, OH: Kent State University Press, 1994).
Junius Henri Browne, *Four years in Secessia: Adventures Within and Beyond the Union Lines, Embracing a Great Variety of Facts, Incidents, and Romances of the War* (Hartford: O. D. Case and Company, 1865).
Robert J. Burdette, *The Drums of the 47th* (Indianapolis, IN: The Bobbs-Merrill Company, 1914).
Sylvanus Cadwallader, *Three Years with Grant*, Benjamin P. Thomas, ed. (Lincoln, NE: Bison Books, 1996).
John Quincy Adams Campbell, *The Union Must Stand: The Civil War Diary of John Quincy Adams Campbell, 5th Iowa Volunteer Infantry*, Mark Grimsley and D. Todd Miller, eds. (Knoxville, TN: University of Tennessee Press, 2000).

Walter B. Capers, *The Soldier-Bishop, Ellison Capers* (New York: The Neale Publishing Company, 1912).

Mary Boykin Chestnut, *A Diary from Dixie*, Isabella Martin and Myrta Lockett Avary, eds. (New York: D. Appleton and Company, 1905).

W. J. Davidson, "Diary of Private W. J. Davidson, Company C, Forty-First Tennessee Regiment," *Annals of the Army of Tennessee and early western history*, (Nashville, TN: A. D. Haynes, 1878).

Jefferson Davis, *The Rise and Fall of the Confederate Government*, Vol. 2 (London: Longmans, Green and Co., 1881).

George W. Driggs, *Opening of the Mississippi; or, Two Years' Campaigning in the South-West. A Record of the Campaigns, Sieges, Actions and March in which the 8th Wisconsin Volunteers have Participated* (Madison, IS: Wm J. Park & Co., 1864).

Arthur Fremantle, *Three Months in the Southern States* (London: William Blackwood and Sons, 1863).

Albert Theodore Goodloe, *Confederate Echoes: A Voice from the South in the Days of Secession and of the Southern Confederacy* (Nashville: M. E. Church, South, Smith & Lamar, 1907).

Frederick Dent Grant, "A Boy's Experience at Vicksburg," *Personal Recollections of the War of the Rebellion*, Military Order of the Loyal Legion of the United States—New York, 3rd Series.

Ulysses S. Grant, "The Personal Memoirs of Ulysses S. Grant," *Memoirs and Selected Letters*, Mary Drake and William S. McFeely, eds. (New York: Library of America, 1990).

Isaac Hermann, *Memoirs of a Veteran who Served as a Private in the 60's in the War Between the States: Personal Incidents, Experiences, and Observations* (Atlanta: Byrd Printing Company, 1911), 103.

Joseph E. Johnston, "Jefferson Davis and the Mississippi Campaign," *Battles & Leaders of the Civil War*, Vol. 3, Robert Underwood Johnson, ed. (New York: The Century Co., 1883).

Joseph E. Johnston, *Narrative of Military Operations, Directed, During the Late War Between the States, by Joseph E. Johnston* (New York: D. Appleton and Company, 1874).

J. B. Jones, *A Rebel War Clerk's Diary*, Vol. 1 (Philadelphia: J. B. Lippincott & Co., 1866).

Jenkin Lloyd Jones, *An Artilleryman's Diary* (Wisconsin History Commission, 1914).

Edward King, *The Great South: A Record of Journeys in Louisiana, Texas, the Indian Territory, Missouri, Arkansas, Mississippi, Alabama, Georgia, Florida, South Carolina, North Carolina, Kentucky, Tennessee, Virginia, West Virginia, and Maryland* (Hartford, Conn. : American Publishing Company, 1875), 307, 311.

S. H. Lockett, "The Defense of Vicksburg," *Battles & Leaders of the Civil War*, vol. 3, Robert Underwood Johnson, ed. (New York: The Century Co., 1883).

James Longstreet, *From Manassas to Appomattox: Memoirs of the Civil War in America* (Philadelphia: J.B. Lippincott Co., 1896).

Mary Ann Loughborough, *My Cave Life in Vicksburg, with Letters of Trial and Travel* (New York: A. Appleton & Co., 1864).

S. C. Miles, *An Epic on "Old Abe," The War Eagle* (Stetsonville, WI: The War Eagle Book Association, 1894).

S. C. Miles, "Capture of Jackson," *The National Tribune.*

Charles Dana Miller, *The Struggle for the Life of the Republic: A Civil War Narrative by Brevet Major Charles Dana Miller, 76th Ohio Volunteer Infantry* (Kent, OH: Kent State University Press, 2004).

Osborn H. Oldroyd, *A Soldier's Story of the Siege of Vicksburg* (Springfield, IL: H. W. Rokker, 1885).

David Dixon Porter, *Incidents and Anecdotes of the Civil War* (New York: D. Appleton and Company, 1885).

David Wilson Reed, *Campaigns and Battles of the Twelfth Regiment Iowa Veteran Volunteer Infantry* (Evanston, IL: 1903).

William T. Sherman, *Memoirs of General W. T. Sherman* (New York: Library of America, 1990).

William T. Sherman, *Sherman's Civil War: Selected Correspondence of William T. Sherman, 1860-1865*, Brooks D. Simpson and Jean V. Berlin, eds. (Chapel Hill, NC: University of North Carolina Press, 1999).

George Steuckrath, "Jackson, Mississippi," *De Bow's Review and Industrial Resources, Statistics, etc.,* J. D. B. De Bow, ed., Vol. 26 (New Orleans: 1859).

Sam Watkins, *Co. Aytch: A Side Show of the Big Show*, 2nd ed. (Chattanooga, TN: Times Printing Company, 1900).

John Melvin Williams, *The "Eagle Regiment,": 8th Wis. Inf'ty. Vols.* (Belleville, WI: Recorder Print, 1890).

Charles A. Willison, *Reminiscences of a Boy's Service with the 76th Ohio, in the Fifteenth Army Corps* (Menasha, WI: George Banta Publishing Company, 1908).

John Russell Young, *Around the World with General Grant*, Vol. II (New York: The American News Company, 1879).

Secondary

Michael B. Ballard, *Pemberton: A Biography* (Jackson, MS: University Press of Mississippi, 1991).

Michael B. Ballard, *Vicksburg: The Campaign that Opened the Mississippi* (Chapel Hill, NC: UNC Press, 2004).

Edwin C. Bearss, *The Campaign for Vicksburg*, Vol 2: *Grant Strikes a Fatal Blow,* (El Dorado Hills, CA: Savas Beatie, 2021).

Robert Patrick Bender, "Evander McNair," *Encyclopedia of Arkansas.*

Linus Pierpont Brockett, *Our Great Captains: Grant, Sherman, Thomas, Sheridan, and Farragut* (New York: Charles B. Richardson, 1865).

Russell K. Brown, *To the Manner Born: The Life of General William H. T. Walker* (Macon, GA: Mercer University Press, 2005).

Stephen Cushman, "Joseph E. Johnston," *Essential Civil War Curriculum.*

William C. Davis, *Jefferson Davis: The Man and His Hour* (New York: Harper Collins, 1991).

Robert W. Dubay, *John Jones Pettus, Mississippi Fire-Eater: His Life and Times, 1813-1867* (Jackson, MS: University Press of Mississippi, 1975).

Brian Johnson, "When Jackson Burned," *Jackson Free Press*.

Stephen Dill Lee, "The Campaign of Vicksburg, Mississippi, in 1863," *Publications of the Mississippi Historical Society*, Vol. III, Franklin L. Riley, ed. (Oxford, MS: Mississippi Historical Society, 1901).

Chris Mackowski, "The Battle of Jackson—and Off to Moscow!" *The Summer of '63: Vicksburg and Tullahoma* (Savas Beatie, 2021).

Donald L. Miller, *Vicksburg: Grant's Campaign that Broke the Confederacy* (New York: Simon & Schuster, 2019).

Brooks D. Simpson, *Ulysses S. Grant: Triumph Over Adversity, 1822-1865*, (New York: Houghton Mifflin, 2000).

Timothy B. Smith, *Champion Hill: Decisive Battle for Vicksburg* (El Dorado Hills, CA: Savas Beatie, 2004).

Timothy B. Smith, "Jackson: The Capital and the Civil War," *Mississippi History Now*.

Addison A. Stuart, *Iowan Colonels and Regiments: Being a History of Iowa Regiments in the War of the Rebellion; and Containing a Description of the Battles in Which They Have Fought* (Des Moines: Mills & Co., 1865).

Craig L. Symonds, *Joseph E. Johnston: A Civil War Biography* (New York: W.W. Norton & Co., 1992).

Terrence Winschel, *Vicksburg: Fall of the Confederate Gibraltar* (Abilene, TX: McWhitney Foundation Press, 1999).

Jim Woodrick, *The Civil War Siege of Jackson, Mississippi* (History Press, 2016).

Steven E. Woodworth and Charles D. Grear, eds., *The Vicksburg Campaign, March 29-May 18, 1863* (Carbondale, IL: Southern Illinois University Press, 2013).

INDEX

Cities are listed as subheads under the state where each is located. For instance, find "Richmond" as a subhead under "Virginia." The exception to this convention are localities in Mississippi, which each have their own entry so as not to get lost under the other "Mississippi" subheads.

Adams, Brig. Gen. John, 35, *35*, 38, 47, 48, 56, 57, 58, 137, 152; grave, *152*

Adams, Col. William Wirt, 122, 123, *123*, 152

Alabama, 53; Mobile, 37; Montgomery, 18, 128

Alabama troops, 35th Infantry, 129

Alexander, Col. Jesse, 101

American Battlefield Trust, viii, xiii, xv, xviii

Anaconda Plan, x

Arkansas, 17; Helena, 45

Arkansas troops, 45

Army of Relief, xi, 24, 126; losses, 130; troop strengths, 17-8, 26, 41, 47, 57

Army of Northern Virginia, 5, 21, 22, 23, 50, 98

Army of Tennessee, 1, 2, 3, 6, 17

Army of Vicksburg, 1, 6, 7

Army of the Cumberland, 23

Army of the Tennessee, xi, 13, 42, 105, 160; losses, 131; troop strengths, 39, 45-6, 57, 59; IX Corps (Parke's), 157; XIII Corps (McClernand's), 45-6, 110; XV Corps (Sherman's), 45-6, 63, 119, 138, 140, 142, 160; XVII Corps (McPherson's), *11*, 45-6, 60, 143, 160

Atlanta, Georgia, 17, 18

Ballard, Michael, 46, 126

Barber, Flavel C., 101

Barksdale, Brig. Gen. William T., 152

Battlefield Park, 136, 140-2, *141, 142*

Battlefield Shopping Center, 136, 139-40, *139*

Bearss, Edwin C., xi, xvi, 49, 62, 84, 85n16, 127

Beauregard, Gen. Pierre Gustave Toutant, 16, 24, 25, *25*, 26, 47

Beauregard, Lt. René, 26, *27*

Bellhaven, 158

Big Black River, xiv, 12, 27, 48, 110, 124, 126

Big Black River, battle of, xiv, xv, xviii

Biser, Capt. Frank, 82

Blair, Maj. Gen. Francis Preston, Jr., 44, *44*, 110

Bland, Slim, 84-5

Boomer, Col. George B., 66, 161

Bouck, Col. Gabriel, 131

Bowman House, 31, 32, *32*, 51, 104, 105, 143-4; as Grant's headquarters, 104, 108, 111; as Johnston's headquarters, 51; ruins of, *127*; site of, 136, 143-4, *144*

Burdette, Pvt. Robert J., 80n5, 81, 82, *82*, 83, 86; and death of artilleryman, 86-7, 107-8

"Burning, The" (short story), 158

Bragg, Gen. Braxton, 1, 6, 7, 17, 22, 23, 49

Breckinridge, Maj. Gen. John C., 18

Browne, Junius Henri, 33n4, 34, 36-7

Bruinsburg, Mississippi, 11, 12

Buckland, Brig. Gen. Ralph, 81, 88, 89, *89*, 106, 113-4, 160

Cadwallader, Sylvanus, 103, 104, 105, 116

Canton, Mississippi, 57

Capers, Lt. Col. Ellison, *74*; wounded, 73

Champion Hill, battle of, xiv, xv, xvi, xviii, 55, 109, 130

Chancellorsville, battle of, xiv, 21, 24, 98, 128

Chesnut, Mary, 5

Chickamauga, battle of, 27

Clinton, Mississippi, xiiv, 44, 46, 58, 60, 114, 143

Colquitt, Col. Peyton, 49, 58, 63, 65, 76, 98, *98*, 131, 162

Confederate Hotel, 32, 117, *118*, 120

convicts, 59, 117

Cooper, Gen. Samuel, 3

Corinth, Mississippi, 40

cotton, 29, 34, *34*, 44, 72, 106; burned, 111, 112, 114

Crocker, Brig. Gen. Marcellus, 65, 66, 67, *67*, 70, 71, *71*, 72, 76, 131, 159

Cromwell, Col. John, 82, 105; killed, 122-3, *122*

Cushman, Stephen, 5

Davidson, Pvt. W. J., 41, 100

Davis, Jefferson, xv, 1, 3-7, *4*, 9, 13, 15, 17, 21, 22, 24, 25, 28, 48, 55, 129, 153; differences in strategy with Joseph Johnston, 19; feud with Joseph Johnston, 3-5, 53, 56, 62n3, 125; health, 20, 22, 27-8; house (Davis Bend), 21; inspection trip to Mississippi, 19, 33-4; statue of, 150; supports Pemberton, 13-6

Davis, Joseph, 4, 19

Davis, William C., 16, 20

Deimling, Maj. Francis C., 65, 67, 73

Driggs, George W., 83, 94, 99, 102

Ector, Brig. Gen. Matthew D., 17, 49

Edwards Station, xiv, 47, 50, 51

Emerging Civil War, xi, xvi

Enterprise, Mississippi, 38

Evans, Brig. Ben. Nathan G. "Shanks," 26

Evers, Medgar and Myrlie, 136, 153; house, *153*

Farquharson, Col. Robert, 58, 66, 67, 76, 161

Florida troops, the lack thereof, 74

Flower, Frank Abial, 95, 96, 102

Fremantle, Arthur, 3, 98

Georgia, 27, 49; Savannah, 26, 47

Georgia troops, 79, 162; 1st Sharpshooter Battalion, 26, 59, 85, 161; 8th Georgia Battalion, 25, 49; 25th Infantry, 26; 29th Infantry, 26; 30th Infantry, 26, 58, 162; 46th Infantry, 25, 49, 58, 162; Martin's Georgia Battery, 26, 79, 83, 85, 162

Gist, Brig. Gen. States Rights, 25, 48, 49, *49*, 57, 162

Goodloe, Albert Theodore, 131

Grabau, Warren, xi, xvi

Grand Gulf, xiv, xvii, 12, 126, 127, 130

Grant, Maj. Gen. Ulysses S., viii, x, xi, xiii, xv, xviii, 8, 9-13, *10*, 18, 21, 23, 24, 27, 30, 48, 50, 53, 55, 112n6, 119, 125, 126, 129, 130, 161; confounds Confederates, 13, 16, 21, 27, 39-40, 47, 51, 124; crosses the Mississippi, xv, 11, 12, 34; decides to move on Jackson, 42-4; intercepts Johnston's dispatch to Pemberton, 109; in Jackson, 104, 108-9, 111-2, 129, 144, 147; and James McPherson, 60, 111; and Joseph Johnston, 62; moves through Mississippi, 12, 18, 21, 35, 39, 40, 44, 110; at Port Gibson, 12, 28, 126, 130; at Raymond, 126, 130; supply lines, 43, 55, 110; and William T. Sherman, 65, 78, 88, 111-2

Grant, Fred, 103-4

Green, Joshua and Thomas, 112, 112n6, 117

Gregg, Brig. Gen. John, 41, 44, 48, 50, *50*, 57, 66, 79, 128, 161; arrives in Jackson, 42; deploys forces, 57-8; misinforms Johnston, 51, 52; at Raymond, 41, 48, 63; withdraws under orders, 98-9

Griffith, Brig. Gen. Richard, 114

Halleck, Maj. Gen. Henry, 11, 12

Hard Times Plantation, 11, 13

Hayes, Rutherford B., 89

Hermann, Isaac, 82, 83, 84, 85, *85*, 87, 100n12

Hewitt, Surg. Henry S., 121

Hill, Maj. Gen. Daniel Harvey, 16, 24

Hillis, Col. David B., 69, 70, 75, *75*, 76, 97, 130

Holmes, Col. Samuel, 65, 66, 68, 70, 74, 97, 161

Hood, Maj. Gen. John Bell, 22, 23, 27, 50

INDEX | 169

Hoskins, Capt. James, 58, 162

Hubbard, Col. Lucius F., 64, 92, 93, 105, 106

Huston, Capt. Littleton W., 75-6

Illinois troops, 123; 2nd Cavalry, 161; 47th Infantry, 81, 82, 91, 105, 107, 121, 160; 93rd Infantry, 161; 114th Infantry, 89, 160; 1st Light Artillery, 83, 86, 161

Indiana troops, 48th Infantry, 159; 59th Infantry, 68, 72, 101, 161; 93rd Infantry, 89, 160

Iowa, 81, 92, 128

Iowa troops, 70, 75, 76; 2nd Battery, 83, 160; 4th Cavalry, 47; 5th Infantry, 161; 10th Infantry, 161; 8th Infantry, 160; 12 Infantry, 64, 106, 113, 115, 160; 17th Infantry, 65, 66, 69, *69*, 70, 74 75, 97, 106, 131, 132, *132*, 159, 161

Iuka, battle of, 81, 121

Jackson (battlefield), vii, ix, 133, 134-159

Jackson, Mississippi (city), ix, xi, xii, xiv, xv, xvii, 1, 12, *12*, 17, 18, 25, 30, *30*, 39, 41, 47-8, 50, 55, 61, 62, 63, 79, 82, 98, 99, 100, 101, 126, 130, 131, 134, 143, 147, 153, 156, 158; as "Chimneyville," 127, *127*; Confederate forces converge on, 1, 25, 26, 27, 28, 48, 49, 57; Confederate evacuation from, 98-101, 108, 125, 126; description of, 30-34, 35, 137, 145, 158; fall of, 125, 129; Federals arrive at, 63, 65, 126; Federal occupation of, 100-23, *102*, *118*; Grant decides to move on, 42-4; history of, 29, 151, 157; as Pemberton's HQ, 12; Joseph Johnston in, 18, 20, 51, 52-3, 61; Joseph Johnston's decides to abandon, 52; in Meridian campaign, 127, 128; overshadowed by Vicksburg, 128, 130; preparations for Grant's arrival, 35-8, 51-2; what ifs of, 130

Jackson, battle of, xi, xiv, xv, xvi, xvi, xviii, 42, 61, *61*, 65-96, *68*, *69*, *80*, *94*, 130; casualties, 131; implications of, 126, 129-31, *134*, 137

Jackson, siege of, xi, xvii, 126, 137, 142, 151, 157, 158-9

Jackson, Andrew, 29, 33

Jackson, Lt. Gen. Thomas Jonathan "Stonewall," xv, xvi, 98, 128

Jackson *Mississippian*, 13, 15, 16, 22, 32

Jastrzembski, Frank, 67

Jefferson, Lt. Col. John W., 104

Johnston, Gen. Albert Sidney, 3

Johnston, Gen. Joseph E., xi, 1-8, *2*, 13, 16, 57, 59, 60, 77, 99, 104, 109, 110, 116, 131, 144, 147, 151, 161; arrives in Jackson, 51; assesses his own performance, 128-9; background of, 3-5; description of, 2-3, 62; differences in strategy with Jefferson Davis, 5, 19, 53-4; feud with Jefferson Davis, 3-5, 53, 56, 62n3, 125; and James Longstreet, 22-3, 27; miscommunicates with John Pemberton, 52-6, 124; in Tennessee, 1, 7, 13, 16, 18; as a threat in Grant's rear, 42, 108, 126; troops love, 101, 126; wounded, 5

Jones, Jenkin Lloyd, 73-4, 105, 106

Jones, John B., 130

Kenderdine, Lt. Harry, 66, 70, 71, 72, 74, 76

Kentucky, Paducah, 79

Kentucky troops, 3rd Mounted Infantry, 48, 59, 79, 161

Lee, Gen. Robert E., xv, 3, 5, 21; resists sending reinforcements to Mississippi, 22-7

Lee, Stephen Dill, 46

Lincoln, Abraham, x, 9, 11, 44, 130

Lingle, Color Sgt. Calvin, 73

Lockett, Samuel H., 53, *53*, 55

Logan, Maj. Gen. John, 66, 76, 100, 130

Longstreet, Lt. Gen. James, 16, 22-3, 24, 27

Loughborough, Mary Ann, 37, 38

Louisiana, 11; Baton Rouge, 131; New Orleans, 121; Port Hudson, 41

Louisiana troops, 4th Infantry Battalion, 26, 58, 162; 12th Infantry, 39

Lundberg, John, 8, 56

Lynch Creek, 79, 80, *80*, 85, 138, 140

Manassas, first battle of, 5

Manship, Mayor Charles H., 36, 147; site of house, 136, 147

Martin, Capt. Lucien B., 101

Martin, Capt. Robert, 26, 59, 79, 83, 162

Matthies, Brig. Gen. Charles, 64, 65, 81, *81*, 85, 88, 113, 160

Maxey, Brig. Gen. Samuel, 49, 57

McClellan, Maj. Gen. George, 6, 35

McClernand, Maj. Gen. John, 39, *42*, 43, 45, 60, 111

McMillen, Col. William L., 90

McNair, Brig. Gen. Evander, 17, *17*, 49

McPherson, Maj. Gen. James, 39, *40*, 44, 45, 60, 61, 62, 63, 67, 68, 70, 78, 82, 83, 97, 99, 101, 129, 143, 160; background, 60; in Clinton, 44, 60; during the battle, 71, 72, 97; leaves Jackson, 110-1; makes first contact, 65; meets with Grant and Sherman, 108-9; misidentified as Sherman, 51, 52, 55

Memphis *Appeal,* 6n7

Meridian, Mississippi, 114

Mexican-American War, 3, 17, 48

Michigan Troops, 2nd Infantry, 158-9

Miles, Pvt. Samuel C., 63, 91, 92, *92*, 93, 95, 99, 118; during occupation, 104, 107, 116, 118-9; and "Old Abe," the War Eagle, 93-6, 93n39

Miller, Charles Dana, 115, 120, 130

Minnesota troops, 5th Infantry, 64, 92, 105, 106, 60

Mississippi, xi, xii, xiii, xv, xvi, xv, xvi, xvii, xviii, 1, 4, 6, 7, 8, 9, 11, 16, 17, 18, 21, 23, 24, 27, 30, 36, 40, 41, 43, 49, 60, 96, 107, 125, 126, 128, 150, 153, 156, 157; governor's mansion, 144-5; history of, 29, 135, 137; Jefferson Davis visits, 19, 20, 33; secession of, 33, 129, 149; slavery in, 33-4

Mississippi Department of Archives and History, 135, 137, 143, 148, 149, 152, 155, 158

Mississippi River, x, xi, xiv, xv, 1, 4, 9, *11*, 13, 19, 21, 24, 39, 53

Mississippi State Capitol, historic, 29, 30, 31, *31*, 51, 101, *102*, 102-4, 107, 119, *127*, 136, 144, 145-6, 147, 149, 150, 153; modern, 154, *154*; see also, "Old Capitol Museum"

Mississippi troops, 85; 14th Infantry, 35, 56, 58, 100, 162; Brookhaven Light Artillery, 58, 162

Missouri troops, 76; 4th Cavalry, 160; 6th Cavalry, 161; 10th Infantry, 65, *69*, 73, 74, 161; 11th Infantry, 105, 160; 24th Infantry, 161; 26th Infantry, 161; 1st Light Artillery, 64-5, 68, 72, 161

Mower, Brig. Gen. Joseph, 81, *81*, 85, 90, 91, 95, 99, 105, 160; as provost guard during occupation, 117-8, 121; withdraws from Jackson, 122

National Park Service, vii, xiii, xvi, 153

National Tribune, 66, 95, 102

navy, xi, *11*, 11-2,

North Carolina, 17, 24

North Carolina troops, 29th Infantry, 17; 60th Infantry, 17

Oaks House Museum, 136, 144, 156

Ohio troops, 62, 76; 4th Independent Cavalry, 161; 20th Infantry, 131; 31st Infantry, 69; 72nd Infantry, 160; 76th Infantry, 114, 116, 120, 130; 80th Infantry, 67, *69*, 74, 75, 161; 95th Infantry, 88, 89, 90, 160

"Old Abe," the War Eagle, 93-6, *94*, 102

Old Capitol Museum, 135, 136, 148-50, *148*, *149*; see also, "Mississippi State Capitol"

Oldroyd, Sgt. Osborn H., 107, 131-3

Overland Campaign, xv

Parke, Maj. Gen. John G., 157

Parrish, L. E., 107

Pearl River, 29, 30, *30*, 38, 115, *115*

Pemberton, Lt. Gen. John, xi, 6, 7, 12, 13, *14*, 15, 16, 21, 24, 26, 39, 41, 43, 46, 51, 57, 99, 108, 110, 125, 131; background of, 13; and Champion Hill, 55, 109, 119; confounded, 47, 48, 50; miscommunicates with Joseph Johnston, 52-6, 124; public mistrusts, 13, 15-6, 126; set up as fall guy, 56

Peninsula Campaign, 5, 6, 62

Pettus, Gov. John, 28, 36, *36*, 37, 38, 128

Pickett, Maj. Gen. George, 22, 23, 26, 27, 35

pikes, 116

Pitzman, Capt. Julius, 88, *88*, 89, 90

Port Gibson, battle of, xiv, xv, xvii, 12, 28, 37, 130

Porter, Adm. David Dixon, x

Powell, David, 45-6

prison bridge, 117, *117*

railroads, 12, 29, 32, 37, 42, 44, 51, 52, *55*, 58, 60, 66, 76, 89, 90, 100, 121, 126, 145; destruction of, 44, 111, 112-4, *115*, 116

Raymond, Mississippi, xiv, 41, 42, 44, 47, 59, 63, 78, 106, 138

Raymond, battle of, xiv, xv, xvi, xviii, 41, 42, 46, 47, 51, 60, 129, 130

Reed, Maj. David, 64, 106, 113, 114, 116

Rosecrans, Maj. Gen. William Starke, 23

Sanborn, Col. John B., 66, 67, 68, 71, 72, 101, 160

secession, 33, 102, 132, 137, 149

Seddon, James, 1, 13, 16, 17, 22, 23, *23*, 24, 26, 27

Seven Pines, battle of, 5

Shaaff, Maj. Arthur, 59

Sherman, William T., 39, *40*, 43, 45, 46, 51, 60, 61, 63, 79, 80, 85, 87, 90, 91, 97, 108, 112, 136, 141, 159; background, 78; confused with McPherson, 51, 52, 55; during the battle, 78, 81, 88, 138, 141; and the March to the Sea, 47; and the occupation of Jackson, 105, 111-2, 117-8, 120-1; postwar friendship with Joseph Johnston, 62n3; makes contact with Confederates, 65; and the Meridian campaign, 114, 127, 128; and the July siege of Jackson, 126-7, 142, 144-5, 146, 147, 159; summoned from Jackson, 119

"Sherman neckties," 113, *113*, *128*

slavery, 33-4, *34*, 37, 38, 102, 137, 154

Smith, Timothy B., xiii, 39, 76, 109n39, 126

South Carolina, 24, 74, 81; Charleston, 25, 48, 57

South Carolina troops, 73; 16th South Carolina, 25; 24th South Carolina, 25, 29, 58, 73, 74n48, 132, 162; Ferguson's South Carolina Battery, 25

Steele, Maj. Gen. Frederick, 90, 112, 119

Stevenson, Maj. Gen. Carter, 41-2

Stevenson, Brig. Gen. John, 77

Symonds, Craig L., 8

"Task Force Thompson," 85, 85n16, 140, 141, 162

Tennessee, 1, 7, 16, 22, 23, 49; Memphis, 6n7, 40, 109, 113; Nashville, 131; Spring Hill, 21; Tullahoma, 1, 13, 18, 25

Tennessee troops, 3rd Infantry, 101, 161; 10th and 30th Infantry (consolidated), 161; 41st Infantry, 41, 100, 161; 50th Infantry, 161; 1st Infantry Battalion, 161

Texas troops, 17, 41, 50; 7th Infantry, 161

Thomas, Col. DeWitt C., 89

Thompson, Col. Albert P., 79, *79*, 80, 84, 87, 99, 139, 162; see also, "Task Force Thompson"

Trans-Mississippi Theater, 9

Trotter, Lt. Alexander, 59

Tuttle, Brig. Gen. James, 78, 79, 81, 83, 88, 90, 91, 112, 119, 160

Two Mississippi Museum, 136, 156-7

United Daughters of the Confederacy (UDC), 142, *162*

Van Dorn, Maj. Gen. Earl, xv, 21, *21*, 22

Vicksburg, Mississippi (city), x, xi, xiv, xvi, 4, 9, 11, 12, 14, 19, 20, 21, 22, 23, 27, 37, 39, 43, 47, 50, 56, 110, 112, 121, 126, 128, 129, 131; as the county seat, xiv; as "the key," x, 9; as the "nail head," 9; Grant's attempts to take, 10, 11; Pemberton ordered to hold city, 53, 55, 124; in relation to Jackson, *12*, 35, 41, 52, 60, 113, 129, 130; surrender of, viii, xiii, 55, 142

Vicksburg (campaign), xi, xii, xiii-xiv, xvii, 10, 18, 43, 109, *125*, 126, 127, 130, 131, 137; as "the Blitzkrieg of the Civil War," 126; Federal troop strengths during, 39, 45-6; Fred Grant during, 103; Sherman's rosy disposition toward, 40

Vicksburg National Military Park, xii, xiii, xvi, 46, 132

Virginia, Richmond, x, xv, 2, 7, 13, 16, 18, 21, 22, 24, 52, 116n14, 128

Walker, Brig. Gen. William Henry Talbot "Shot Pouch," 26, 47, 48, *48*, 57, 58, 59, 98, 129, 162

Watkins, Pvt. Sam, 3

Watts, Sgt. John, 91

Welty, Eudora, 136, 157-8; house, 157, *157*

West Point, 35, 53, 60, 78

White, Kristopher D., xiii, xv, xviii, 40

Williams, John Melvin, 92, 94, 95

Willison, Pvt. Charles A., 114, 120, 121

Wilson, Lt. Col. James H., 111

Wisconsin, 93

Wisconsin troops, 63, 83, 92, 99, 116, 119; 6th Artillery, 72, 161; 8th Infantry, 91, 92, 93, 95, 101, 102, 104, 105, 116, 119, 160; 18th Wisconsin, 130, 160

Woodrick, Jim, ix, xvii, 127, 135, 137, 138, 142, 146, 149, 150, 158

Woodworth, Stephen, 52, 102, 145

Wright House, 58, 65, *68*, 69, *69*, 73, 74, 132, 136, 143

Yerger, Maj. William, 122

About the Author

CHRIS MACKOWSKI Ph.D., is the editor-in-chief and co-founder of Emerging Civil War and the series editor of the award-winning Emerging Civil War Series, published by Savas Beatie.

Chris is a writing professor in the Jandoli School of Communication at St. Bonaventure University in Allegany, NY, where he also serves as associate dean for undergraduate programs. Chris is also historian-in-residence at Stevenson Ridge, a historic property on the Spotsylvania battlefield in central Virginia. He has worked as a historian for the National Park Service at Fredericksburg & Spotsylvania National Military Park, where he gives tours at four major Civil War battlefields (Fredericksburg, Chancellorsville, Wilderness, and Spotsylvania), as well as at the building where Stonewall Jackson died.

Chris has authored, co-authored, or edited nearly thirty books on the Civil War, and his articles have appeared in all the major Civil War magazines. Chris serves as vice president on the board of directors for the Central Virginia Battlefields Trust and also service on the advisory board of the Civil War Roundtable Congress and the Brunswick (NC) Civil War Roundtable, the largest in the country.